Putting Students First

Putting Students First

How Colleges Develop Students Purposefully

Larry A. Braskamp
Loyola University Chicago

Lois Calian Trautvetter
Northwestern University

Kelly Ward
Washington State University

Anker Publishing Company, Inc.
Bolton, Massachusetts

Putting Students First
How Colleges Develop Students Purposefully

ISBN 1-882982-94-0

Composition by Jessica Holland
Cover design by Jennifer Arbaiza Graphic Design

Anker Publishing Company, Inc.
563 Main Street
P.O. Box 249
Bolton, MA 01740-0249 USA

www.ankerpub.com

Library of Congress Cataloging-in-Publication Data

Braskamp, Larry A.
Putting students first : how colleges develop students purposefully / Larry A. Braskamp, Lois Calian Trautvetter, Kelly Ward.
p. cm.
Includes bibliographical references and index.
ISBN 1-882982-94-0
1. Holistic education. 2. Education, Humanistic. 3. Education, Higher—Aims and objectives. I. Trautvetter, Lois Calian. II. Ward, Kelly (Kelly Anne) III. Title.

LC990.B73 2006
378.1'98—dc22

2005029637

Contents

About the Authors

Larry A. Braskamp received his B.A. from Central College and his M.A. and Ph.D. from the University of Iowa. In 1967, he joined the University of Nebraska–Lincoln as a professor in the Department of Educational Psychology, where he received a Distinguished Teacher Award. After serving at Nebraska as assistant to the chancellor, he came to the University of Illinois at Urbana-Champaign in 1976. There he held a number of administrative positions, including associate vice chancellor for academic affairs, director of the Office of Instructional and Management Services, and acting dean of the College of Applied Life Studies. He was dean of the College of Education at the University of Illinois at Chicago (UIC) from 1989–1996. From 1996–1997, he was on leave from UIC to serve as the executive director of the Council for Higher Education Accreditation. In 1997–1998, he was professor of policy studies in the College of Education and a faculty fellow in the International Center for Health Leadership Development at UIC. Currently he is professor emeritus of education at Loyola University Chicago, where he served as senior vice president for academic affairs, and senior fellow at the Association of American Colleges and Universities.

His research interests include the role of church colleges in American higher education and the role of faculty assessment in faculty development and organizational decision-making. He is the coauthor or coeditor of six books, including *Assessing Faculty Work: Enhancing Individual and Institutional Performance* (Jossey-Bass, 1994), *Evaluation of Campus Services and Programs* (Jossey-Bass, 1987), and *The Motivation Factor: A Theory of Personal Investment* (Lexington Books, 1986), and has published more than 100 research articles and papers.

Lois Calian Trautvetter is associate director for Northwestern University's Higher Education Administration and Policy Program and lecturer in the School of Education and Social Policy. She received her Ph.D. in higher education administration from the University of Michigan, her M.S. in polymer chemistry from Carnegie Mellon University, and her B.A. in chemistry from The College of Wooster. She teaches college student development theory and research methodology courses. Her research interests include faculty and professional development issues such as productivity, enhancing research and teaching, motivation, and new and junior faculty. She is also interested in the role of church colleges in American higher education as well as professional development for K–12 teachers to improve math and science teaching, gender issues, and females in science. She participated as a researcher in the past two postsecondary national centers for education funded by the Department of Education (Office of Educational Research and Improvement) and has written book chapters and articles on faculty. She also has patents as a chemist in the coatings and resins industry.

Kelly Ward is associate professor of higher education at Washington State University. Her research interests are in the areas of faculty work, including balancing teaching, research, and service; faculty involvement in the community; and balancing work and family for those on the tenure track. She is also interested in campus and community engagement, service-learning, and policy issues related to equity and diversity. Dr. Ward has held faculty and administrative positions at Oklahoma State University and the University of Montana. She earned her Ph.D. in higher education from Penn State University.

Foreword

The term *faith-based* has acquired some heavy baggage in today's politically polarized society. It's become a code word for religious ideology, and, like many other people in the mostly secular world of higher education, I don't much like ideology. I find it dangerous. I believe that the only role for ideology in the academy is as an object of skepticism, an opportunity to challenge accepted truth with cross examination and debate. For this reason I've had, I admit, a prejudice against *faith-based* institutions. I've regarded them as places where parents send their kids to protect them from a world full of heresy and temptation—places where "liberal education" is regarded with suspicion, bounded by religious orthodoxy, or, in extreme cases, is nowhere to be found.

With this book Larry Braskamp and his colleagues Lois Trautvetter and Kelly Ward have demonstrated just how wrong-headed I've been. This book, and the study upon which it is based, is a valuable service to the academy, giving us a rich and evocative portrait of how 10 faith-based colleges, and by extension scores of others like them, are in fact promoting the kind of liberal learning that more secular institutions can only wish for. These institutions are not just fostering "engagement" (as if simply being engaged in something, anything, were enough), they are helping students define their vocation, their calling, something to be engaged *about*. The more evangelical of these colleges hope their students will deepen their faith, to be sure; but they eschew indoctrination. For them, having students engage in self-examination and critical self-reflection is what is most important. They care about the process. (The reader will not, in fact, find the term *student learning outcomes* anywhere in this book, thank goodness.) For these colleges holistic student development is not just a matter of helping students learn a set of marketable skills, it is a matter of helping them learn how to live.

How refreshing this is! Some years ago I had an informal conversation with several members of the English faculty of a public comprehensive university. The topic turned to the challenges of teaching freshmen students. I was ready for the usual litany of complaints about how students today can't think and can't write and don't care. To my surprise these faculty were concerned about something else entirely. One, speaking for the others, said, "The problem isn't that we need to force students out of their conventional ways of thinking. They've grown up in a postmodern world. They come to college not really knowing what matters, and they hunger for an anchor, something that will give their lives meaning." And then she said this (a literal quote): "What they need is a course called Values 101." The wistfulness of their conversation told me that this group didn't expect to see Values 101 on their campus anytime soon.

What these faculty were wishing for was not that their institution should decide what values to impart and then teach those values. What they wanted was what Braskamp and his colleagues found on the campuses they visited: "a rigorous, intellectual challenge in which the head and the heart are integrated in the search for truth, meaning, and fulfillment." The authors of *Putting Students First* have captured the essence of these colleges in a manner that is accessible and inviting to the secular world. One can read this book from the perspective of a public research or comprehensive university or community college and come away with ideas for creating environments that honor both skepticism and meaning-making, exploration and wholeness.

And isn't that, in the end, what college should be for?

Jon F. Wergin
Professor, Ph.D. Program in Leadership and Change
Antioch University

ACKNOWLEDGMENTS

This book is a collaborative effort, to be sure. Without the assistance, encouragement, and insights—the investment—of literally hundreds of students, faculty, academic leaders, and professional staff in student affairs and ministry at scores of church-related colleges and universities, this book would not exist.

As the authors, we are primarily serving as transcribers and interpreters of what we think are the key characteristics of a segment of American higher education—church-related colleges. These institutions have often been overlooked in conversations about the diversity and quality of American higher education. We have learned that these are unique places, and the hospitality of these colleges is just one example of their special character and identity. Furthermore, those laboring at these institutions were more than willing to talk with us about their work and their lives so that we could tell the larger communities of their investment in students.

This book is based on a research project that extended over a three-year period. The project initially received support from chief executive officers of eight church college associations: Bob Agee, Charles Currie SJ, Monika Hellwig, Steve Johnson, Gary Luhr, James Noseworthy, Arne Selbyg, and Donald Thompson. With their help, we were able to receive completed surveys on faculty expectations, assessment, and development from more than half of the nearly 500 chief academic officers of these colleges. More than 30 chief academic officers took the time to be interviewed by phone or invited us to their campuses to tell their stories of faculty involvement in student development. These academic leaders provided us with considerable insights about the life of faculty from their perspectives. We were also fortunate to have the counsel of several chief academic officers who spent two days in Chicago to react to these findings and to help us better communicate the results and plan for the next phase of the project. They are: David Gillespie, Anne Lippert, James Pence, Fred Pestello, Carla Sanderson, John Smarrelli, and Richard Stroede.

The second major phase of this project included in-depth site visits to 10 colleges: Bethune-Cookman College, Creighton University, Hamline University, Hope College, Pacific Lutheran University, The College of Wooster, Union University, the University of Dayton, Villanova University, and Whitworth College. The willingness and support of the chief academic officers and their staffs in making the visits efficient and productive cannot be overstated. James Boelkens, Ian Crawford, John Johannes, James Pence, Fred Pestello, Tami Reid, Carla Sanderson, Alan Silva, Ann Taylor-Green, and Christine Wiseman—we acknowledge and respect their professionalism. They allowed us to retain our own conclusions and interpretations, even when they differed and had good reason to do so.

Throughout the three years, we received considerable encouragement, challenges, and support from a number of people—colleagues at work, reviewers of sections of the book, excellent conversationalists about the topic, and supporters of the project, especially in its early stages. The following individuals contributed in many ways: Timothy Austin, Robert Benne, Charlotte Briggs, Robert Brown, Arthur Chickering, Jon Dalton, Sister Ann Ida Gannon, Charles Glassick, John Haughey SJ, Jennifer Haworth, George Kuh, Ralph Lundgren, David Myers, KerryAnn O'Meara, Linda Salchenberger, Donald Schmeltekopf, James Wellman, Jon Wergin, Terry Williams, and Randall Zachman. Again, we were fortunate to have a dedicated group of scholars come to Chicago for two days this summer to provide a critique of the draft. Charles Blaich, David Guthrie, R. Eugene Rice, Clara Sanderson, Steven Schomberg, Elizabeth Tisdell, and William Weston quickly formed a "community of challenge and support" and provided us with feedback from which to revise the manuscript—at times dramatically. It is a better book because of their input.

This project was funded by the Lilly Endowment, Inc. and the John Templeton Foundation. Their financial support and interest in advancing a national dialogue about the contributions of faculty in fostering student development is greatly appreciated. We also wish to acknowledge the wise counsel of Chris Coble and Arthur Schwartz, whose personal involvement in this project made it more focused and useful.

We end on a more personal note.

For Lois, this was a chance to observe college communities investing in students, mirroring some of my college student experiences. This project has allowed me to reflect on the many faculty members and administrators who were putting students first, especially my chemistry professor and advisor, Theodore Williams, who helped to guide me in my "big and worthy questions" and analyze the water content and elemental analysis of cataractous eye lenses. In addition to the many mentors and colleagues that continue to invest in my learning, I also had the encouragement and role models of my parents, Sam and Doris Calian, who both have personally invested their time, talent, and energies in guiding many students in theological education for more than 40 years. I am also extremely grateful to my supportive husband Dennis and my three wonderful but energetic children—Rachel, Paula, and Caleb—who encouraged me, even though it was a sacrifice at times. In the future, I hope that each of my children will experience a college that is committed to developing students purposefully.

For Kelly, this project brought to light the unique place that church-related colleges occupy in the higher education landscape. I appreciate the opportunity to "hang around" and take in all the great conversations and interactions happening on the campuses in the study. I'm grateful to all the students, staff, and faculty that invited me to be part of the conversation so I could better understand what it means to put students first. I'm also grateful to countless colleagues who have engaged in conversation with me throughout the past year as I teased out what it meant to work and study at a church-related college. I thank Susan Gardner for all her support in helping me organize the details of the project. As always, I must acknowledge my family for just being there.

For Larry, I was challenged and supported in this project in numerous ways. I was continuously reminded of the wisdom of Reverend John Boyle, who strongly advocated that "we are expected to judge, but to not be judgmental." Throughout this project, I had the good fortune of being able to play tennis in the early morning hours with Paul Gignilliat, who helped me keep a perspective on the project and appreciate the power of routine, discipline, and friendship deepened by competing. My two sons, David and Steven, were their usual supportive selves. Moreover, David provided me with good company during the summers, assisting in the analyses and being a helpful critic. I end by acknowledging the patience and support of my wife Judi, who allowed me to break a promise that I would not write another book, because she knew it would only again lead to self-absorption. Since it did turn out to be the most difficult and intellectually challenging piece of scholarship of my career, she had to be and was even more supportive. She deeply understood that this book is for me more than an achievement or product. It is a reflection of my life, my vocation.

We end with a collective note and perspective. We all found this project to be a very enlightening, challenging, and rewarding experience. Each of us has grown immensely in writing this book, partly because the task of understanding how colleges help students in their sense-making is not easy. However, we witnessed firsthand many faculty and staff investing themselves in others—and it was rewarding to observe. We now welcome you and your colleagues to also purposefully invest in students.

Introduction

We wrote this book with a perspective in mind. We argue that an effective and ideal undergraduate college education is one that centers on holistic student development, including the search for meaning and purpose in life. Who a student is and becomes during college, as well as what a student does during college, is important to us. The title of this book, *Putting Students First*, is meant to stress three overarching themes. First is the intentionality of colleges as they guide students to become what the college thinks and believes is a desired end for students. Colleges and universities are mission oriented and act intentionally; that is, they educate and work with students on purpose, not accidentally. They intentionally invest in students.

Second, colleges develop students in ways that recognize and build on the student's purpose in life, intellectually and morally. Intentional colleges create environments that center on purpose, helping students reflect on such questions as—Who am I? What are my goals in life? How do I want to make a difference with my life? Addressing questions about the "good life," as we discuss it in this book, is a part of student development. Thus life is not only about financial achievement and professional success, but living a life that is fulfilling and meaningful. The real joy in life often comes from addressing challenges that fulfill one's purpose in life. Aristotle refers to a distinction between making a living and living a life—endeavoring to develop our full and highest potential as human beings. One can live a good life by being good and excellent at what one is called to be as a person. Worldly success as some like to measure it—materialism, money, power—may not always be the final criteria to judge the quality of one's life (Gomes, 2002; O'Toole, 2005). It may require one to experience hardships, disappointment, challenges beyond what one wishes for, and to carry the burdens of others. For some, it requires a commitment that is intimately linked to their religious faith or a higher rule or principle. Putting students first thus also calls for a holistic view of student development that encompasses cognitive, psychological, moral, ethical, and faith development.

This leads to the third theme of the book: Faculty play an integral role in fostering student development. When we say "putting students first," we are not advocating a student-centered environment that meets all of its students' demands. Rather, we emphasize that faculty and other influential adults in the lives of students (e.g., professionals in student affairs and ministry, coaches) need to be involved to foster student development, holistically.

We present the findings, conclusions, and interpretations based on our study of 10 church-related colleges: Bethune-Cookman College, Creighton University, Hamline University, Hope College, Pacific Lutheran University, The College of Wooster, Union University, University of Dayton, Villanova University, and Whitworth College. These colleges not only desire to help students be successful—a goal of most educators today and of importance and value to be sure, but they were selected since we wanted to learn how colleges think, plan, and behave in preparing students to live their lives as well as making a living. While the selected colleges are very supportive of preparing students to be vocationally competitive locally, nationally, and internationally, they argue for an education to be more. We selected colleges that intentionally assist students to ask and "struggle" with the fundamental questions in life while they are in college.

We selected colleges to represent a range of church and religious histories and current commitment to a particular religious or faith perspective. Some deliberately advance a certain faith or church denominational perspective and others can be classified as being quite secular in their perspective. We did not select a homogeneous group of colleges according to a set of criteria, but rather chose colleges to represent the diverse group of the 500 colleges that were founded by one of ten church denominations (Braskamp, 2003). These colleges were selected because they have been successful in preparing students to enter into graduate and professional schools, for their recognition of being closely affiliated with their church or legacy, and/or for being a good place to work. We did not select a set of institutions to represent an "ideal college" or to establish a standard of excellence.

All of these colleges have three characteristics in common. First, they put students first in their mission, even though all pursue other goals such as research and service to the community. Second, they all share a commitment to educate students holistically. All share a desire to assist students in their faith development, as we define it in this book. Thus they differ from many excellent colleges who put students first, including many of the public, community, and regional colleges and for-profit institutions and research universities, but primarily for professional preparation. Third, these colleges, shaped by their history of being founded by a church denomination, still deal with educating students that include a religious and faith dimension in educating their students. At some of the colleges, it is a daily challenge and for others it arises occasionally, brought about by special events or an external circumstance.

Organization of the Book

In Chapter 1, we set the context for putting college students first and highlight four major tensions and challenges that leaders and faculty need to address as they create campus environments that foster holistic student development. Chapter 2 describes the methodology, design, and framework for our work.

In Chapters 3 through 6, we present data-based summaries of the different dimensions of the campus environment in which leaders can invest to effectively foster student development. We organize the campus environment using what we call the 4C framework: culture, curriculum, cocurriculum, and communities in and beyond campus. These 4Cs encompass and represent different aspects of a college campus that enable faculty and others to become involved in student development. The 4Cs are a schema to help faculty and campus leaders organize and rethink strategies to foster holistic student development. The 4C framework is a heuristic device to help campus leaders think practically about investing in students. Each of these chapters concludes with questions intended to create campus conversations around the issue of holistic student development.

Chapter 7 presents an overview of the findings, employing three major characteristics to describe a student-invested college community, and calls for consideration and action for campus communities in an effort to put students first. We also include a set of questions for each characteristic that we hope will be a starting point for campus conversations at many colleges and universities.

Given the emerging student body and the changing role of faculty, this book is timely for higher education. It will be of interest to campuses and their constituents that strive to put students first and to support faculty and other staff in this endeavor. Although we chose to study church colleges, our analyses, recommendations, and insights gleaned from the study can be useful to campus leaders from all types of colleges and universities—large and small, secular and religious—that put students first. We hope leaders of any college interested in student development will find similar results and perspectives on their campuses and will join us in a dialogue on how to most effectively put students first.

1 Putting Students First

"I came here to invest in my students."
—Faculty member, Whitworth College

"If there is one sentence everyone around here can quote it is 'Creighton University exists for students'."
—Dean, Creighton University

Introduction

These remarks and many more like them directed us to title this book *Putting Students First.* Faculty and administrators at the colleges we studied made their perspectives on student development known by the way they talk of investing in students. Generally they use language that reflects a view of student development that is holistic and encompasses the intellectual, moral, psychological, and faith development of students. They press students to acquire knowledge *and* to develop a life of purpose; they challenge students to obtain *and* improve competencies and to "know themselves"; and they encourage students to engage the world *and* to probe the relevance and power of religious commitments and perspectives and their shortcomings. In all the colleges in the study, educational leaders were most interested in investing in students such that they might live holistically.

This book is based on our desire to learn more about why and how colleges foster students' holistic development. In doing so, we addressed questions such as—What do colleges desire students to become? What skills and patterns of behavior do students need to learn and develop? What are the learning and developmental goals of a college education? How do colleges create and sustain a campus environment that fosters holistic student development? How do members of the campus community—faculty, staff, and administrators—contribute to the development of students by who they are as well as what they do? When we posed such questions, we heard repeatedly about the concept of putting students first. In a nutshell, faculty involvement in students' holistic development is about investment—faculty dedicating themselves more fully to the totality of student life, colleges making an investment (literally and figuratively) in students as whole beings, and students themselves becoming personally invested in their collegiate experience. This book is about how faculty and their colleagues in student affairs, administration, and ministry put students first.

The purpose of this chapter is to set the stage for the book by addressing the following questions: Why is it important to put students and their development first? Who are today's students? Who is developing these students? In what context is holistic development occurring? Why study church-related colleges and universities?

Why Is It Important to Put Students and Their Development First?

Increasingly, educators refer to the importance of all dimensions of student development, not just formal learning. After all, Aristotle argued that minds must be developed in relation to the use of reason and character must be developed in relation to passions and feelings. Leaders of colleges and universities organize their campus activities—curriculum, cocurricular events and programs, culture, and collaborations with organizations external to the campus—in ways that they consider develop students most effectively. Moreover, they organize educational endeavors by first considering desired ends: "What do we wish students to be and to become," often framed in terms of student learning and developmental goals. For some, the desired end of an education is mastery of skills needed for a specific career; for others, moral and civic responsibility is emphasized; for still others, character development and religious formation are primary. In varying degrees of intentionality, colleges pay attention to the interior lives of students—values, spirituality, identity, purpose, and meaning—and the exterior lives of students—observable patterns of behavior.

In this book, we use the term *student development* to include our spectrum of holistic student learning and developmental goals. Defined in these terms, this spectrum includes the following dimensions:

- Vocational knowledge and skills
- Professional practices and skills
- Intellectual, critical thinking, and reasoning
- Academic, disciplinary, and interdisciplinary knowledge
- Physical well-being
- Social responsibility
- Civic and political responsibility
- Moral and ethical responsibility
- Personal values and character
- Self-awareness, self-authorship, and identity
- Spirituality
- Faith and the practice of faith
- Religious commitment, conviction, and worldviews

Student development defined to include a wide array of learning and developmental goals is not a new way of viewing the college experience. Holistic student development was the core of the mission of the first colleges and universities in America; they were founded to assist young men and women to be persons of character and integrity. "The early American college did not doubt its responsibility to educate the whole person—body, mind, and spirit; head, heart, and hands" (Boyer, 1987, p. 177). Almost a century ago, professionals in student affairs viewed college life in terms of an inclusive student-centered perspective. The American Council on Education (1937/1994) referenced that the student personnel point of view "emphasized the importance of education for the whole student" (p. 76). Recently, attempts to develop the "whole student" have been advocated in terms of fostering civic and moral engagement of college students. For example, the Kellogg Commission (1997) states, "The biggest educational challenge we face revolves around developing character, conscience, citizenship, tolerance, civility, and individual and social responsibility in our students" (p. 26–27).

In terms of combining intellectual and character development, Boyer (1987) argued,

> We need educated men and women who not only pursue their own personal interests but are also prepared to fulfill their social and civic obligations. And, it is during the undergraduate experience, perhaps more than at any other time, that these essential qualities of mind and character are refined. (p. 7)

Dalton, Russell, and Kline (2004) state, "American higher education has always been deeply invested in the development of character as an outcome of the college experience. The notion of character is imbedded in the most basic concepts of liberal education, public service, and student development" (p. 4). Colby, Ehrlich, Beaumont, and Stephens (2003) argue that "moral and civic learning should be a central goal for both liberal and professional education" (p. xi). The Association of American Colleges and Universities (2002) proposes five learning goals that colleges need to fulfill if they are to educate American students. The goals are analytical and communication skills; understanding and experiences in the disciplines; intercultural knowledge and collaborative problem-solving skills; civic, social, and personal responsibility; and integrative thinking and problem solving. In short, they advocate a practical liberal arts education, an education in which students begin to apply their knowledge and understanding to be good workers and citizens.

Most recently, Nathan Hatch (2005), former provost at Notre Dame University and new president of Wake Forest University, called for an education of college students that links intellectual and moral development. In his review of Catholic higher education in recent decades, he concludes, "What is evident is a commitment to the holistic nurturing of students—body, mind, and spirit" (Hatch, 2005, p. B16). In summary, the academy as a whole has always advanced the dual goals of forming and informing students while in college.

Who Are Today's College Students?

Holistic student development calls for us to understand the students we are developing. The college student today cannot be described easily and simply. No single generalization does justice to the complex and conflicting portrayal. They are increasingly commuter-based, older, and diverse in gender, race, and ethnicity; for example, more than 40% of students are 25 years or older. Since most research in higher education is focused on traditional-age undergraduate college students, including our own, the findings that we offer may be inadequate if applied to the total college population today.

The most common image of traditional-age college students today is the one known as the *millennials*, referring to students born after 1982. They are described as

> smart, ambitious, incredibly busy, very ethnically diverse and dominated by girls [sic]. . . . They make decisions jointly with parents ("co-purchasing" a college) and believe in big brands (with "reputation"

> counting for a lot). And they are numerous, very intent on going to college, and have very demanding parents. (Howe & Strauss, 2003, p. 4)

Their "helicopter" parents are always hovering over campus ready and willing on a moment's notice to become involved in the affairs of their son or daughter. With the help of technology like cell phones and email communication, they are never far away. Parents have also become more vocal in their expectations to college leaders and faculty.

In addition, these students are highly involved in extracurricular activities, very focused on getting high grades, facile in using technology in their studies and work, somewhat conventional by their desire to have boundaries and order in their environment, and very accepting and tolerant of racial and other forms of diversity (Howe & Strauss, 2003). Millennial students are also portrayed as compassionate and caring individuals, often immersed in service and community activities. They reflect in part the larger current societal context.

In recent years, secular and church-related institutions have noticed that students have become increasingly interested in religion and spirituality. Students are looking to religion, sometimes broadly defined, for meaning, comfort, and certitude—a place to stand and rest (Fish, 2005). An ethnographic study of campus religious life concludes that "It is possible that young people in American culture have never been more enthusiastically engaged in religious practices or with religious ideas" (Cherry, DeBerg, & Porterfield, 2001, pp. 294–295). This revival of religion and spirituality represents the most vibrant aspect of pluralism today on campus (Nash, 2001). Students want to associate with faculty who are willing to assist them in their search for a life of meaning (Chickering, 2003). Further, students have returned to tradition and ritual as suggested by Howe and Strauss (2003), and thus come to college with certain predispositions such as favoring the "teaching of values, including honesty, caring, moral courage, patriotism, democracy, and the

Golden rule" (p. 5).

Recent research on more than 100,000 first-year students at 236 colleges and universities supports the notion that today's college students are showing a high interest in spirituality (Higher Education Research Institute [HERI], 2005). According to this survey, entering college students are interested in spirituality (80%), searching for meaning in life (76%), using their beliefs for guidance (69%), discussing life philosophies with friends (74%), attending religious services (81%), believing in God (79%), and praying (69%). Overwhelmingly, these students, who are not always sure what they believe, are very interested in grappling with big questions like the meaning of life and looking for ways to incorporate these spiritual and religious questions into their college experience. Two in three want their institutions to play a role in their spiritual and emotional development. One-half of the students say it is essential or very important that colleges encourage their personal expression of spirituality. Students also desire exploration of meaning in life and values more often in the classroom. Only about half of the juniors said they were satisfied with how their college experience provided "opportunities for religious or spiritual development," and more than six in ten students stated "their professors never encourage discussions of spiritual issues" (HERI, 2003). Similar findings about student interest in spirituality were found in the National Survey of Student Engagement (2004).

A number of students have recently been described as missionary students who have a cause—they are on a mission to make America a different and better place to live (Riley, 2005). Deeply influenced by their backgrounds in a faith, often described as evangelical in nature, tone, and purpose, these students are not timid about what they want to accomplish in life and even how they should carry out their calling to serve others in response to their commitment to their God. Religion, faith, and spirituality are a part of their lives. Moreover, they are active as members of a community, such as a church or social organization with a faith dimension, and comfortable sharing their personal lives with others. Missionary students are clear about their role and purpose in society. They subscribe to Aristotle's argument that in order to be truly fulfilled in life they must apply the fruits of their personal development to meeting some of the needs of others.

Regardless of the image that guides how we think about today's college students, all students are asking fundamental life questions (Denton-Borhaug, 2004): Who am I? How can I use my talents to make a contribution? What is the purpose of a college education? Students are expressing interest in finding meaning in their lives and dealing with questions of values and faith as part of a college education. They seek purpose as part of their college experience and look for ways to reconcile career goals, personal passions, and intellectual pursuits. In short, they are interested in obtaining a holistic education.

Who Develops These Students?

Many people on college campuses—student personnel administrators, peer leaders, administrators, and faculty—are involved in the holistic development of students. It is faculty, however, who may have the most significant influence on college students. According to Pascarella and Terenzini (1991, 2005), relationships among students and faculty form the core of the college experience. Faculty are considered important contributors to mentor and advise students, to shape the future of academic programs for them, and to prepare future citizens for the challenges of a complex world (Colby et al., 2003; Parks, 2000). In recent years, however, a widening gulf between students and faculty has occurred (O'Meara & Braskamp, 2005; Rice, 1996). This gulf can be described in terms of changing expectations of faculty contributions. The most often mentioned major responsibilities of a faculty member are teaching, research, and service. Virtually all agree that teaching is at the heart of what it means to be a faculty member. As modern roles for faculty have evolved, another part of the faculty role that is clear—at least to those on the "inside" of academe—is research. Faculty are creators of knowledge and information (Altbach, 1995; Boyer, 1990b). The service role of faculty, however, is less clear (Berberet, 2002). Likewise, expectations for faculty beyond the classroom and in student life are unclear. This shift in expectations is due, in part, to the professionalism of higher education over the past decades. Professionals in student affairs and ministry have assumed many of the functions—counselor, advisor, and directors of spiritual life—that faculty once assumed.

What, then, is the role of faculty in students' holistic development? How can faculty work in the classroom be reconciled with faculty work beyond the classroom? What is expected of faculty today? To some, faculty have become too detached, impersonal, experts from afar, and they have been accused of not being adult role models to students (Chickering, 2003). However, a desired image of a faculty member is emerging, with a portrayal consisting of words like fellow learner in the communal search for truth, good company, fellow traveler, encourager of dialogue rather than one-way communicator of truth, spiritual mentor, and the guide on the side (Baxter Magolda, 2002; Palmer, 1998; Parks, 2000). Fostering holistic student development is not an abstract or impersonal task. Faculty need not leave their "person hat at the door" (Tisdell, 2003, p. 254) of the classroom if education is to be transforming in holistic ways. If faculty are to help students explore their vocation, "faculty likely will need to re-think their roles . . . it will take determined, steady work to convince faculty members that they are, first, teaching young people, and secondly, teaching some aspect of the field they profess" (Lagemann, 2003, p. 11).

The challenges and obstacles to do so are many, however. Faculty are not being rewarded for working with students (Diamond, 1999; Huber, 2002). Faculty in all institutional types are spending more time engaged in research and writing compared to 20 years ago, activities that may be insufficient to foster the kind of student development and learning that emphasizes coherence and mutuality among learning goals (Dey, Milem, & Berger, 1997; Milem, Berger, & Dey, 2000). Over the last two decades, faculty workloads have significantly increased (O'Meara & Braskamp, 2005). While faculty and administrators see a need for greater involvement with students, they are unclear about how to proceed, since most faculty have not been trained or socialized in graduate school to relate to students in a more holistic way. Graduate schools are not yet preparing their students to be primarily teachers and mentors (Austin, 2002, 2003). Faculty are also fearful of being intrusive in the private lives of students, first amendment rights, and that they will be viewed as too sympathetic and thus soft on students (Astin & Astin, 1999).

Nevertheless, faculty members welcome the opportunity to view their role in terms of who they are as well as what they produce. Today, faculty desire a blending of the professional with the personal (Rice, 2002). Younger faculty want to be more connected to the world in which they live. They do not like separation between their personal and professional lives, and they desire to define their work in terms of vocation and a sense of a social commitment to society, although they may not use these words to describe and define their lives as academics (Braskamp & Wergin, 1998). Most faculty want to lead an integrated and balanced life that cannot be compartmentalized into their work—their professional life—and their personal life, but they often see this dream shattered in the first years of their career (Lindholm, 2003; Wergin, 2003; Wulff, Austin, & Associates, 2004).

In What Context Is Holistic Development Occurring?

The college context is important to consider as we think about faculty involvement in student development. We frame this context in terms of tensions that can shape and influence faculty in their work with students. We focus here on four major tensions:

- Mission and market
- Individual gain and the public good
- Faith and knowledge
- Compartmentalization and community

We present these tensions as a way to frame the context of college campuses, not for resolution or elimination. Instead, we see them as critical and creative tensions that can energize the college community in fostering holistic student development.

Mission and Market

In a consumerist and market economy, college campuses are often focused on preparing students for the workforce and their careers, without much consideration for preparation for life. Do colleges and universities exist to assist students in "making a living and living a life?" Should college be the place and time when students ask questions about purpose in life and their future roles as citizens, family members, and professionals?—Why am I here? What is my purpose?—Do colleges frame these bigger life questions with careerist responses?

Many colleges, especially those with a legacy rooted in the religious and/or a strong liberal arts tradition, face a tension in being true to their historical roots and the centrality of a liberal arts education on the one hand, and in being responsive to the desires of college students and their parents with strong market place interests on the other. Such expansion is a considerable deviation from their historic mission of serving predominantly traditional-age students in a residential environment. How can an institution balance meeting the challenges of adult students, offering courses online, and developing students holistically, which seems to require face-to-face interaction? Such tensions can lead campuses to ask—What is our mission? What do we stand for in terms of educating our students?

Individual Gain and the Public Good

One does not need to read much about higher education today before encountering commentary about the role of higher education in perpetuating the self-serving nature of our society, including college students. Commitment to the public good has diminished in favor of individualistic views of self in society (Putnam, 2000). Is college more than the means to assist students to get into professional and graduate schools and prepare them for a good career? Is higher education primarily a commodity in the national and international economies? Many campuses have responded by creating or invigorating civic and moral education initiatives focused on students (Cantor & Schomberg, 2003; Colby et al., 2003) and looking more seriously at faculty roles and rewards and how they perpetuate individualistic or community-oriented ends (Boyer, 1996; Ward, 2003). Not only are colleges expected to prepare students to be active and moral citizens in society, but institutions themselves are expected to be good neighbors, partners, and leaders in addressing the social ills and the economic challenges of our society. Colleges are to be responsible stewards of the traditional academy and responsive to the current challenges of the world in which we live (Braskamp, 1997). But what does it mean to be a good neighbor? How can an institution partner with other social institutions like churches, social service agencies, and K–12 schools without forfeiting its primary purpose of providing a good education to students and pursuing knowledge through research and scholarship, and being a helpful critic to society through its commitment to the "good" for society?

Faith and Knowledge

Sloan (1994) contends that the coexistence of faith and knowledge in the academy historically has resulted in one overshadowing, if not altogether obliterating, the other. If Sloan's argument has merit, the efforts of church-related institutions can easily be characterized as tense. On the one hand, they desire to acknowledge the import of their religious traditions and, on the other hand, they are committed to scientific curiosity and methodology. Practical questions that capture this tension abound—Can a student both think critically and be committed to a particular faith perspective? Will a faculty member fairly represent multiple perspectives if he or she is persuaded by a particular religious perspective? Is there such a thing as a Catholic view of economics or a Lutheran view of politics? Are all faith perspectives equally valid, acceptable, or beneficial? Does acknowledging a religious tradition impede academic freedom? (Diekema, 2000). Are postmodernist, feminist, and gay perspectives as much "faiths" as Jewish, Muslim, or Christian perspectives? Is the pursuit of knowledge ever neutral? How do we know what we know? (Buchanan, 2005). Church-related colleges and universities—more than any other type of institution—wrestle with these kinds of tensions precisely because they simultaneously endorse the academic enterprise and their religious heritages. In addition, they respond to the tensions between faith and knowledge differently, largely based on the particular contours of the historic and contemporary manifestations of their respective religious traditions.

Compartmentalization and Community

During the past century the student affairs profession has become more professionally-minded, has assumed more responsibilities in American higher education, and has become increasingly interested, proactive, and diligent in its role in fostering both academic (*intellectual* is the word now most often used by these professionals) and personal development. Professionals in student life have always been highly active in advocating living-learning environments to foster integration of learning and development, emphasizing that student development encompasses both cognitive and affective domains. They have consistently desired to work collaboratively with faculty in fostering intellectual, ethical, and personal development of students (American Association for Higher Education, American College Personnel Association, & National Association of Student Personnel Administrators, 1998; Brown, 1972, 1996; Hamrick, Evans, & Schuh, 2002).

Student affairs and academic affairs, though increasingly collaborative, are still compartmentalized. Leaders and faculty create and maintain their college community built on the premise that faith is a subjective, emotional, and private matter and the search for truth and understanding is a public and rational undertaking. Faculty by and large have given the responsibility of fostering the social, religious, ethical, and religious formation of students to the professionals in student affairs and campus ministry (Miller & Ryan, 2001; Oakley, 2002; Wolterstorff, 2002). Colby et al. (2003) conclude, “Much of the explicit attention to moral and civic learning on today’s campus is provided in extracurricular programs rather than in the classrooms” (p. 33). Faculty members for the most part have endorsed this, since it still allows them to stay relatively uninvolved in the personal lives of students. Faculty recognize that this is dangerous work, but faculty and campus leaders also have come to realize that they can best engage and energize students if they develop relationships of trust within community. Academic leaders have increasingly begun to expand the goals of higher education to include a fostering of the heart as well as cultivating the life of the mind; that is, a view of student development that is holistic and goes beyond learning. What remains a challenge is the manner of educating students holistically in this era of pluralism and diversity.

In summary, colleges with a goal of educating undergraduate students cannot escape the pressure and demands of the larger academy and society. Context matters, and it is the response to these tensions and challenges that often defines how a college is serving the larger society and its students. Today, colleges feel pulled between preparing students for career and for life, fostering faith and intellectual purpose, being responsible stewards of the traditional academy and being responsive to the current and immediate needs of society, and creating a sense of community among faculty and students so the bigger questions of life can become part of an education.

Why Study Church-Related Colleges and Universities?

Currently, church and faith-related colleges and universities account for more than 900 of the more than 6,500 institutions of postsecondary education in the United States. These colleges and universities historically have been an important sector in the diversity of higher education in America (Dovre, 2001). Almost all of the private colleges began with a religious mission, but over the past century considerable secularization of these colleges has occurred (Marsden, 1994). During the past three decades a significant number have neglected to build on their historical religious roots. With the turn of the new century, however, there seems to be a renewed interest in the appeal, visibility, and contribution of these colleges and universities to our society (Dykstra, 1999; Guthrie & Noftzger, 1992; Mahoney, Schmalzbauer, & Youniss, 2001; Wolfe, 2002). Dovre

(2001) notes the "reality of the renaissance which is being expressed by and experienced by many religious colleges in America" (p. 18). But with opportunities come challenges. The first sentence of Diekema's (2000) book, *Academic Freedom and Christian Scholarship*, is, "The dawning of Christianity's third millennium finds many Christian colleges and universities in a search for identity" (p. 1).

These institutions are rich in tradition and differ in a number of significant ways from their secular counterparts. They have the potential to revivify the life of the mind and influence the heart of students by considering the importance of faith (Dykstra, 1999; Mahoney et al., 2001). Given the emerging interest in church-related colleges and universities and their long legacy of developing students holistically, there is a new urgency to understand the current realities that define these institutions, clarify the challenges they confront, provide thoughtful analyses of the issues they encounter, and offer examples of their practices. These institutions have as their mission to incorporate faith, spirituality, and religion and prepare students for lives of moral and intellectual complexity. Church-related colleges and universities also have a history of addressing such fundamental issues as the role of faculty and how their curricular, pedagogical, leadership, and governance practices reinforce integration of faith and learning. Since these institutions are dedicated to the development of the whole student, they provide the types of settings from which we can learn how to educate students to be well prepared for their careers and to develop students holistically as good citizens and persons of character.

We are not advocating a return to higher education's clerical roots or issuing a plea for more faith-related colleges. Our intention is not to proselytize or to suggest a greater role of religion in higher education, but to argue that studying the colleges that we did has implications for all college campuses with respect to investing in students' holistic development. Due to size, religious affiliation, mission, and related factors, what may be effective at these campuses may need to be adapted for other types of campuses, especially those that are public, secular, larger in size, and less residential. For this reason, we highlight themes, principles, and strategies, and provide examples from the colleges to illustrate a point. We agree with Terenzini, who has concluded that the "search of 'best practices' is misguided" (Barefoot, Gardner, Swing, & Terenzini, 2005). Instead, he argues for research to provide principles and touchstones against which leaders on a campus can evaluate and judge an idea, plan, strategy, or practice.

At times we point out how the colleges are different. The distinctions that exist among the colleges are many, profound, distinguished, and very important. However, we most often deliberately focus on the commonalities of these diverse colleges and universities, given their common end to focus on holistic student development. Each tries in unique ways to achieve the goal of fostering holistic student development, although these processes are defined uniquely by each college. Moreover, faculty members, as we hope to show, play different roles in fostering holistic student development at these colleges.

Summary

We have been impressed, excited, and encouraged by how each institution we studied deliberately and intentionally addresses the challenge of fostering holistic student development. It is in these attempts that we have looked for common themes. Although it is more often the case that smaller colleges and universities glean their information from larger universities, we believe that other colleges and universities can learn from the summaries, findings of policies, programs, and practices at these selected church-related colleges. It is our intent to provide analyses of the findings of these campuses by putting them into a broader context, applying a theoretical interpretation and perspective of them, and offering some suggestions and recommendations for consideration. Since all campuses have to deal more forthrightly with religion and spirituality, church-related institutions can be used as a starting point for all types of campuses to think about their commitment to putting students first more holistically and the unique role of faculty in achieving this goal. We now turn to a more in-depth explanation of the research design of the study, including a methodological and theoretical overview.

2 Conceptual Framework and Design of the Project

"Here faculty develop students to have a sense of purpose, not from a religious point of view, but from a spiritual and philosophical perspective."

—Faculty member, Bethune-Cookman College

Introduction

A holistic view of student development conveys learning and development and the integration of intellectual and academic learning with personal development. In our view, assisting students to think in terms of who they are as well as what they do is one of the major goals of college. Putting students first means helping students contribute to a pluralistic society while still guiding them to discover a self-identity and purpose based on being informed and wise thinkers. It also means assisting students to understand and appreciate different perspectives and to begin forming their own perspectives. All colleges presume an environment that encourages students to explore, imagine, and ask fundamental questions about life, but students at some colleges do so in an environment that has a dominant or several prevalent worldviews and perspectives. In these colleges, students are expected to ask good questions, but they do so at a place that is willing to suggest "answers" about the most fundamental issues of life.

In this chapter, we offer theoretical bases for fostering a holistic view of student development. We present a conceptual framework, Personal Investment Theory, that guided our research and propose a 4C schema—culture, curriculum, cocurriculum, and community—to organize our findings. We also share the project design, including brief descriptions of the 10 colleges and universities where we conducted the case studies on which this book is based.

Theoretical Bases for Holistic Student Development

In the past two decades, scholars of human development have argued for a more holistic approach to helping students develop that enables students to manage the complex problems and "dissonance" of today's world (e.g., Baxter Magolda & King, 2004; Colby, Ehrlich, Beaumont, & Stephens, 2003). Educating students holistically is being reemphasized, incorporating an appreciation for diverse beliefs and backgrounds. It is based on the assumption that exposure to different worldviews, cultural or religious, leads to greater complexity in thinking and development (Cantor & Schomberg, 2003). Many student development theorists point out that students move from lack of awareness of identity, through a period of confusion and exploration, to an internally defined perspective. Students take into account their race, ethnicity, or sexual orientation in developing their views of themselves and the world (Hamrick, Evans, & Schuh, 2002). Recognizing this complexity is important to understanding how a sense of self or self-awareness forms.

Historically, the study of student development has heavily concentrated on the cognitive or intellectual dimensions (Baxter Magolda, 1992; King & Kitchener, 1994; Perry, 1968). More simplistic stages of cognitive development involve concrete thinking and what might be called blind belief, whereas later, more complex levels of cognitive development reflect an ability to consider knowledge grounded in context, deriving judgments from personal experiences, evidence from other sources, and from the perspectives of others. Some developmental theories also take into account psychosocial stages or levels of college student development (Chickering & Reisser, 1993). For example, using developmental theory to plan student activities suggests different programming for first-year students' needs than for seniors' needs.

Although cognitive development is necessary for moral development, more is involved. Students develop by exposure to multiple perspectives and contradiction. When they see that authorities can disagree, students understand the possibility that they can learn in ways beyond collecting authorities' ideas (Baxter Magolda, 1992; King & Kitchener, 1994; Kohlberg, 1976). Further, students in college begin to achieve self-authorship—the ability to define their own beliefs, identities, and relationships. Students become less reliant on external authority and assume personal ownership and responsibility for their lives (Baxter Magolda & King, 2004; Kegan, 1994).

Faith, Spirituality, and Student Development

Faith development often has not been included as a component of a holistic approach to student development in past decades. However, the terms *spirituality*, *religious commitment*, *character*, and *faith* are now common in the literature on college student development (e.g., Astin, 2004; Chickering, Dalton, & Stamm, 2005; Jablonski, 2001; Love, 2002). Our perspective on fostering student development includes the development of faith as well as of spirituality and religious commitment. We use the word *faith* most often when we are referring to a student's nonrational, affective, and ethical dimensions, often conveyed as the "interior" of one's life (Astin, 2004). We use the word *faith* as James Fowler (1981) has defined it: "The ways we go about making and maintaining meaning in life" (p. xii). We also like the definition of Peter Gomes (2002): "Faith is not some abstract theological construct . . . it is the way by which people make sense of a world that alone, on its own terms, makes no sense" (p. 256).

In general terms, faith development refers to an intentional effort to make meaning of one's life or to obtain a higher stage of moral reasoning (Fowler, 1981). Faith implies a hope and trust in someone or something larger than oneself—transcendence beyond one's own being. Faith

> has both affective and cognitive dimensions . . . [it] is the ground of ethics and the moral life. Faith is intimately linked with a sense of vocation—an awareness of living one's life aligned with a larger frame of purpose and significance. (Parks, 2000, p. 26)

Developing an authentic spiritual identity involves moving away from or deeply questioning one's childhood religious tradition and authorities to which one has been exposed, in favor of a critical-reflective process. This kind of development typically occurs among college students (Fowler, 1981; Parks, 2000; Tisdell, 2003), particularly when faculty and staff acknowledge it as a viable aspect of students' holistic development and attempt actively to contribute to the process.[1]

Faith can include religious commitment, in the sense that faith and the practice of faith are intractably connected.

> Religion describes a social entity . . . religions are defined by their boundaries. There are group members and nonmembers, prescribed and proscribed behaviors, and characteristic beliefs. Spirituality is a central concern of religions, but not the only concern. A religion can also involve important social, political, and economic goals. (Miller, 2004, p. 13)

Religion is often associated with a set of beliefs about supernatural power(s) (e.g., God, supreme force) and one's relationship to a transcendent source or being. Religion also often has a set of doctrinal standards or dogma and involves public expression, worship, and sacraments. It implies community with shared beliefs, commitments, and convictions, a community for celebrating and mourning the lives of others (Marty, 2000).

Faith also incorporates spirituality, which is turning inward to oneself but in such a way as to experience "an encounter with otherness" (Palmer, 1990, p. 5). It is full of affect but is not merely an emotional quest. It touches the core of our being and existence. It helps one to know oneself (Astin, 2004) and to claim an authentic identity, cohesiveness, integration, and wholeness (Tisdell, 2003). Spirituality in its broadest definition is finding one's purpose in life through inner reflection and introspection and taking action. It includes prayer and meditation, commitment, performance, and connections with others. To be spiritual in the fullest sense is to feel and act as a person who desires to be a part of the larger society. While spirituality is often viewed as individualistic—there are not church creeds and rituals to adopt to be spiritual—being spiritual is to be socially and morally responsible (Dalton, Kline, & Tull, 2004; Tisdell, 2003); it is part of being human. Arthur Schwartz (2001) concludes his discussion of spirituality this way: "Perhaps at the core of 'spirituality' is a mysterious relationship that opens our hearts to questions of intimate meaning and ultimate truth" (p. 35). Spirituality reflects a sacredness of life and an acceptance and celebration of the mystery of life. As reported by Gallop and Lindsay (1999), the American adult population has become much more interested in being spiritual over the last half of the previous century, with more than eight in ten now expressing a desire to develop spiritually.

In our view of student development, we want to stress the interrelationships among faith, religious commitment, spirituality, and intellectual dimensions. All are involved in a student's journey of finding purpose and meaning, but colleges vary in how interrelated they are and can be. Some argue that finding meaning is independent of religious commitment. We do, however, emphasize that college student experiences need to be viewed holistically. A student comes to college, goes to class, and engages in the life of the campus as a person, not as one dimension. In our focus on student development, we stress connections among intellectual, social, and faith dimensions of student development and how students as individuals develop within campus and societal contexts. In short, we are referring to the matters of the heart as well as the mind when we use the term *holistic student development.*

We also propose that a holistic approach to student development helps to prepare students to address life's big questions as well as the great challenges they are likely to witness as college students and as citizens in a pluralistic world (Parks, 2000). We call for a more holistic view of student development because we believe such a view will help students to develop their convictions and to articulate their views of the world and their places in it. We also argue that a college education can include preparing students to examine and develop further the purpose for their lives, meaningful relationships, and the value of giving back to society. In our view, colleges have a responsibility to assist students with all aspects of their development.

Not all colleges and universities want to be this inclusive in their education. For example, in a speech to incoming first-year students at the University of Chicago, Professor Andrew Abbott (2002) gave this advice:

> For you as individuals, your responsibility to yourselves for finding education is not limited to the cognitive matters to which the university . . . largely restricts itself. You need to become educated in morals and emotions as well. And in those areas, I am sad to say we do not really provide you with anything like the systematic set of exercises in self-development that we provide on the cognitive side. So you are on your own. (p. 8)

We do not think that students should be "on their own" to develop in ways other than intellectually in college. Thus, we take a broad view of student development, one that considers the emotional, moral, and cognitive sides. Such a view conveys both learning and development and the integration of intellectual and academic learning and personal development. Using an inclusive spectrum of student learning and developmental goals, each college in the study, in its own unique way, creates a campus environment that fosters the holistic development of students.

Student Development and the Church-Related Context

Much of the common literature on student development is based on three fundamental assumptions:

> 1) Knowledge is inductive, not deductive, that is, it is derived from the structured observation of experience; 2) The individual is primary and the community is a voluntary association of individuals; and 3) Individual choice is the fundamental social value. . . . In contrast, the Catholic intellectual tradition suggests a different set of assumptions as follows: 1) Truth is deductive, not inductive, that is, it is derived from fundamental principles that interact with and interpret experience; 2) Human beings are fundamentally social beings and not isolated individuals; and 3) The common good, not individual choice, is the fundamental social value. (Estanek, 2001, p. 47)

We mention this at the outset to underscore the notion that holistic student development is not a monolith. More importantly, it is also not value-neutral. Rather, the fundamental beliefs and values that an institution holds shape the ways in which it conceives of and enacts its efforts to help students learn and develop. In the context of our study, it seems reasonable to expect that church-related colleges will understand and practice holistic student development in some ways that may differ from large public universities.

One example helps to illustrate the point. Kathy Storm (2004), vice president of student affairs at Whitworth College, basing her arguments in part on the work of Niebuhr (1951), prefers to think of a college education in terms of educating students for adaptation *and* for transformation. She argues that students need to be prepared to face all of the world's challenges with a sense of humility and self-understanding that one cannot fully control one's destiny in life. Life is more than conforming to and then controlling society; it is a journey of transforming society based on a set of beliefs and commitments—a worldview—which may not be fully aligned with the dominant societal values and practices. Success, as defined by the larger society, may not be selected as the desired standard to use in guiding one's life and making career choices. Like the Catholic traditions, this perspective stresses service to others, and not necessarily accepting the dominant normative societal perspective. In sum, the "good life" is not universally defined in the academy or in our society.

Conceptual Framework: Personal Investment Theory

Since we stress holistic student development, including a wide spectrum of learning and development dimensions, we have selected a theory—Personal Investment Theory—that allows us to include both the inner and exterior lives of students and the sociocultural environment. It is built on the centrality of meaning and stresses the importance of the relationship among a student's sense of self, patterns of behavior, and the nature of the sociocultural context that is the college environment (see Figure 2.1); as such, Personal Investment Theory refers to the entire process of student development.

FIGURE 2.1
Application of Personal Investment Theory to College Student Development

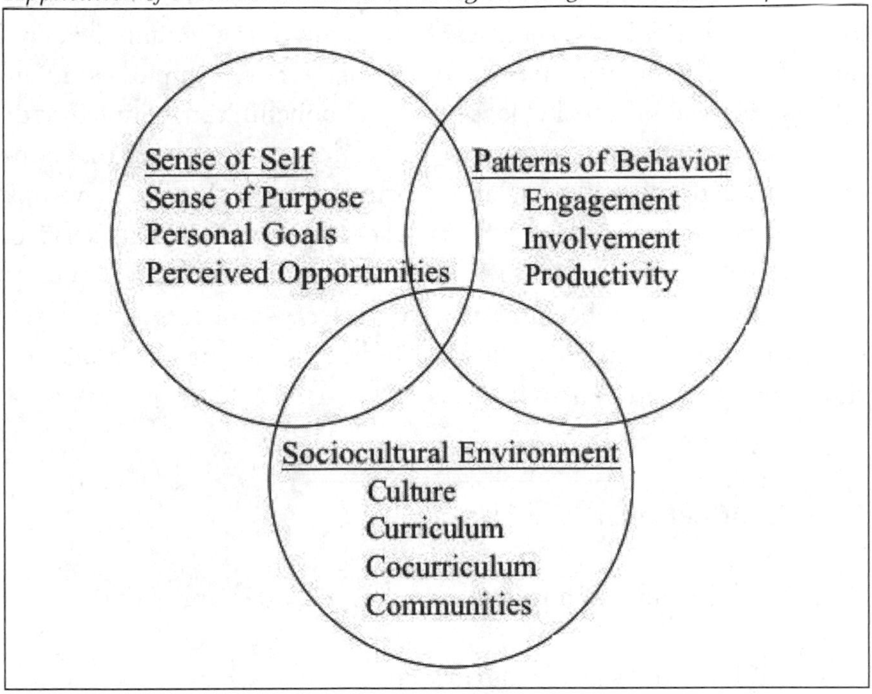

Personal Investment Theory admittedly has a metaphorical character to it, as noted by McKeachie (cited in Maehr & Braskamp, 1986, p. xv). To be personally invested is to be involved, motivated, persistent, engaged in activities, intense and intensive, and to have patterns of behavior that are noticeable to others. Students are personally invested when they use their time, talents, gifts, and energy to achieve something, whether in the classroom, the residence hall, on the playing field, in a social service agency, or among family and friends. Students make choices about where to spend their time and what to become engaged in, "depending on the meaning these activities have for them" (Maehr & Braskamp, 1986, p. 62).

Just being busy is not enough for an authentic and purposeful life. Rather, an authentic and purposeful life involves connecting s and behaviors; a student selects activities that reflect lf and purpose. It is this connection between who one is an ne does that is critical to understanding human development; both need to be fostered and developed. For example, a student who is involved in tutoring local grade-school children, coupled with his or her commitment to serve and a campus environment that supports this activity and offers an opportunity for reflection, develops differently than a student who is just simply involved in service. Colleges can fulfill the goal of fostering holistic student development by helping students be introspective, reflective, and self-knowing, since one's inner life is an integral part of investing one's talents, time, and energy into activities.

Patterns of Behavior

Kuh, Kinzie, Schuh, Whitt, and Associates (2005) argue that

> What students *do* during college counts more in terms of what they learn and whether they persist in college than who they are or even where they go to college . . . the time and energy students devote to educationally purposeful activities is the single best predictor of their learning and personal development. (p. 8)

We concur that how students spend their time is a major factor in the development of students. We also stress, however, that colleges need to give credence to who a student is, paying particular attention to fostering this element in student development.

Sense of Self

Sense of self consists of personal goals, perceived opportunities, and a sense of purpose. We stress the importance of the sense of self, since it is an essential antecedent of one's patterns of behavior. Sense of purpose and commitment bring a discussion of student development closer to a view that incorporates identity, faith, values, spirituality, and religion. Persons invest their time, talents, and energy into what they do because it is meaningful to them, which is mediated by their sense of self, sense of purpose, and personal goals. Not all students have similar personal goals and values such as power, affiliation, accomplishment, and recognition (Maehr & Braskamp, 1986). Students engage in activities partially based on their sense of self—their personal goals and sense of purpose; they largely invest to fulfill a perceived purpose in life (Braskamp & Hager, 2005). As such, student development in our view is not a linear, rational, or strictly cognitive process. Instead, students rely on their college experiences as ways to develop meaning, to make choices, to take action, and to develop their talents and gifts.

In this process of developing a sense of self, students often reflect on two major questions—Who am I? How do I best make a contribution to this world? The first question is one of self-identity and self-identification; developing a sense of self—What is my purpose in life? The second question can also be thought of in terms of students wondering how best to serve others and how best to use their gifts to fulfill their goals and dreams and make the world a better place.

We argue that the process of developing a sense of self can be viewed in terms of vocation. Vocation is not an activity or event, but rather a lifelong journey of becoming who one is and expressing oneself in life. Vocation entails asking the two questions "Who am I" and "How can I best contribute?" Neafsey (2004) states,

> According to Jung, the process of 'becoming what we are' involves both self-discovery and self-expression. Individuation requires, first of all, that we become conscious of who we are, and then calls upon us to find ways to actualize or express the unique truth of who we are within the unique circumstances and realities of our life situation. (p. 15)

Lagemann (2003) has noted that students are at a loss about a career at graduation, a consequence of not really concentrating in college on what they want to do with their lives. She argues that higher education should pay more attention to helping students develop their vocation in life: "The word vocation implies more than earning a living or having a career. The word vocation implies having a calling: knowing who one is, what one believes, what one values, and where one stands in the world" (p. 8). These perspectives are closely aligned with the conceptual framework of Personal Investment Theory (Braskamp & Hager, 2005; Haughey, 2004). Vocation can be viewed in terms of investing one's time, talents, and energy in one's daily life, whether it be in school, work, recreation, family, or community.

Campus Environment

The environmental aspect of Personal Investment Theory emphasizes the other major antecedent to students' patterns of behavior—students' sociocultural environment. The sociocultural environment plays an important role in influencing one's perceived opportunities. The mores and norms of a person's sociocultural environment help a person decide which alternatives are acceptable to pursue. It provides a set of expectations and opportunities for the members. Beyond the particular sociocultural dimensions of one's environment, it is important to note that other people in one's social networks and those in society at large also play roles in identifying acceptable and unacceptable beliefs and behaviors.

As shown earlier in Figure 2.1, we portray this environment in terms of a 4C framework—culture, curriculum, cocurriculum, and community. The campus environment represents a significant element of a student's sociocultural environment and influences a sense of self and engagement. One does not personally invest talents, time, and energy in a vacuum; rather, one is influenced by the expectations of others and the opportunities available.

In summary, Personal Investment Theory encompasses not only the college student, but, equally important, the campus environment where the college student dwells. It stresses the connections between being and doing within a sociocultural context, which for students is the campus community. Personal Investment Theory helps us to see the importance of the relationship between a student's sense of self and engagement, using a choice- and decision-oriented interpretation of why people behave the way they do and why they engage in activities. Thus, colleges need to consider who students are and who they will become, as well as what they do. The theory also helps us to understand why faculty and other campus leaders invest their time, talents, and energy into what they do. By investing in students, they can find purpose and meaning in their own development.

Project Design

Since 2002, we have been actively involved in the research project "Fostering Student Development through Faculty Development" funded by Lilly Endowment, Inc. and the John Templeton Foundation. The initial goal of this project was to understand better how faculty are expected to foster student development from the perspective of the chief academic officers (deans, vice presidents for academic affairs, provosts) of church-related colleges. More than 250 academic leaders of nearly 500 colleges that are affiliated with, associated with, or are members of one of ten church denominations completed the survey. The number of completed surveys by colleges affiliated with their denomination is listed in Table 2.1. These institutions represent the Carnegie Classification proportions quite well, so the representativeness of the more than 900 church-related colleges is sufficient in our view.

Table 2.1
Colleges by Denomination Participating in the Survey

Denomination	Surveyed	Returned	%
Southern Baptist	49	38	78
Catholic	194	94	48
Episcopal	9	5	56
Presbyterian USA	65	28	43
Lutheran	42	25	60
United Church of Christ	30	10	33
United Methodist	93	49	53
Reformed Church	6	6	100
Total	*488*	*255*	*52*

At the end of the first year, we also conducted phone and face-to-face interviews with more than 30 deans and provosts from those institutions that responded to the survey. The purpose of the interviews was to gain insight into the sociocultural context of student development, particularly the role of the faculty in the college community. The following is what these academic leaders conveyed to us in their survey responses and interviews:

- *Faculty are expected to have personal qualifications and attributes that make them role models to students.*
- *Faculty are free to express personal perspectives but should not force them on others.* Faculty sharing their personal perspec-

tives to colleagues is different from sharing personal beliefs and values with students. Deans and provosts noted the potential danger of faculty being too influential on students in personal matters, due to their status and authority.

- Two-thirds of the chief academic officers gave considerable or strong importance to the statement, "*Faculty are to assist students in their search for personal ethics and moral development*," but less than one in three gave the same importance to "*Faculty are to assist students to develop their spirituality, faith, and religious perspectives.*"

- *College leaders try to communicate the college's mission and identity effectively*. But they also respect and encourage diverse values and personal faith traditions of faculty, students, and staff. They want to avoid promoting a culture of conformity.

- *The college mission and identity is salient in how a college hires and assesses faculty*. Almost all colleges have a rigorous screening and elaborate review process for hiring faculty to maximize "fit" and support the mission of the institution.

- *A historic church and religious legacy varies among colleges by denomination—and within the colleges of a particular denomination.* The range is from a strong institutional reliance and support of a religious or church tradition to indifference. At many colleges, faculty are expected to help build a new legacy, whereas in others, they build on the historical legacy of the college.

- Faculty are to be involved in research and scholarly activities, but *deans and provosts more highly value faculty being scholarly in their work rather than producing scholarly work.* However, at research universities faculty are also expected to be productive researchers.

- *All colleges have faculty development programs* (e.g., orientation programs, mentoring). Most programs are intended to promote and foster faculty as lifelong contributing members of the community. These programs are necessary because many faculty are often ill-prepared from their graduate study to immediately and effectively contribute at these colleges.

In-Depth Site Visits

In the second year, we conducted in-depth case studies of 10 campuses to learn more about the role of faculty, other staff members, and administrators in guiding students in their development. The 10 colleges where we conducted intensive site visits represent diverse institutions. We deliberately selected institutions that reflect different regions, church denomination, size, affinity with the sponsoring church, mission, and adherence to a dominant religious or faith perspective. The site visits generally lasted two to three days and involved interviews with faculty, administrators in campus ministry and student affairs, students, the chief academic officer, and the president about their roles in fostering student development. To learn more about the campus, its mission, and its approach to working with students, we also reviewed relevant documents (e.g., curriculum requirements, promotion and tenure guidelines) and observed campus events (e.g., lectures on relevant topics). The colleges we visited are listed in Table 2.2.

TABLE 2.2
Colleges of Intensive Campus Visits

Institution	Denomination	State	# Students	# Undergraduate	% Residential	% Denomination	% Non-White
Bethune-Cookman College	Methodist	Florida	2,895	2,895	60	82 Protestant	92
Creighton University	Catholic-Jesuit	Nebraska	6,723	3,888	57	63 Catholic	17
Hamline University	Methodist	Minnesota	4,544	1,997	41	53 Protestant	14
Hope College	Reformed Church	Michigan	3,112	3,112	79	69 Protestant	7
Pacific Lutheran University	Lutheran	Washington	3,600	3,000	50	67 Protestant	6
The College of Wooster	Presbyterian	Ohio	1,800	1,800	95	51 Protestant	13
Union University	Baptist-Southern	Tennessee	2,800	1,950	65	62 Protestant	11
University of Dayton	Catholic-Marianist	Ohio	10,000	6,500	95	70 Catholic	10
Villanova University	Catholic-Augustine	Pennsylvania	8,700	6,200	65	83 Catholic	14
Whitworth College	Presbyterian	Washington	2,200	2,000	56	76 Protestant	14

We did not select colleges that have a "Programs for the Theological Exploration of Vocation" grant from Lilly Endowment, Inc. (www.PTEV.org). However, seven of the ten colleges have been awarded grants of up to $2 million to establish a four-year program on their campuses that assists students in "examining how faith commitments relate to vocational choices"—defined by each of the participating institutions—and to encourage students to become church leaders, including full-time ministry. Our goal in this project was not to evaluate the success of these programs (which were at different stages of development and implementation), but to exam more holistically how the colleges in their entirety foster student development. We wanted our findings and analyses to be generalizable to all types of institutions educating undergraduates and not limit the scope of the project to those that have special external programs focused on vocation. These programs are being evaluated by others (e.g., Drummond, 2005), and their impact at 88 colleges and universities is considered to be significant (Dykstra, 2003). For this book, we have underplayed the role of these projects by design.

Bethune-Cookman College

Founded in 1904, Bethune-Cookman College is a historically black, United Methodist Church-related college offering baccalaureate degrees. The mission of Bethune-Cookman is "to serve in the Christian tradition the educational, social, and cultural needs of its students—traditional and nontraditional—and to develop in them the desire and capacity for continuous intellectual and professional growth, leadership, and service to others." While related to the Methodist Church, only 8% of Bethune-Cookman's students report themselves as Methodist. Located in Daytona Beach, Florida, Bethune-Cookman enrolls more than 2,600 students and employs approximately 160 full-time faculty, giving Bethune-Cookman a 17:1 student to faculty ratio.

Creighton University

Located in Omaha, Nebraska, Creighton University, "one of 28 Jesuit colleges and universities in the nation, enrolls more than 6,000 students annually in nine schools and colleges, including medicine, dentistry, and law." Founded in 1878, Creighton University is a "Catholic and Jesuit comprehensive university committed to excellence in its selected undergraduate, graduate and professional programs." A full-time faculty of 667 members ensures Creighton's 14:1 student to faculty ratio.

Hamline University

Founded in 1854 by Methodist pioneers, Hamline University is located in St. Paul, Minnesota, and was the first institution of higher education in the state. Enrolling more than 4,000 undergraduate, graduate, and law students, Hamline has more than 300 faculty members and a 13:1 student to faculty ratio. Maintaining an affiliation with the United Methodist Church, the university's stated mission is "to create a diverse and collaborative community of learners dedicated to the development of students' knowledge, values, and skills for successful lives of leadership, scholarship, and service."

Hope College

Hope College was founded in 1851 and is located in Holland, Michigan. Currently enrolling more than 3,100 students, Hope's student to faculty ratio is 13:1. The mission of Hope College is "to offer, with recognized excellence, academic programs in liberal arts, in the setting of a residential, undergraduate, coeducational college, and in the context of the historic Christian faith." Hope College is affiliated with the Reformed Church in America.

Pacific Lutheran University

Founded in 1890 by Norwegian Lutherans living in the Puget Sound area, Pacific Lutheran University (PLU) is located 40 miles south of

Seattle in Tacoma, Washington. Enrolling more than 3,600 undergraduate and graduate students, the mission of PLU is to "empower students for lives of thoughtful inquiry, service, leadership, and care for other persons, for the community, and for the earth." Closely affiliated with the Evangelical Lutheran Church of America, only 28 % of its students are identified as Lutheran. PLU describes itself as a comprehensive university that is "committed to the integration of liberal arts studies and professional preparation" as it offers both bachelor's and master's degrees in multiple subject areas. A faculty of 242 full-time and 70 part-time members serves the student body, which translates into a 14:1 student to faculty ratio.

The College of Wooster

A liberal arts college, The College of Wooster is located in Wooster, Ohio, approximately 55 miles southwest of Cleveland. Founded in 1866, Wooster is best known for "an innovative curriculum that emphasizes independent learning," where "each Wooster senior creates an original research project, written work, performance or exhibit of artwork, supported one-on-one by a faculty mentor." Originally founded and owned by a synod of the Presbyterian Church, Wooster became independent in 1969 but still chooses to maintain a voluntary relationship. The mission of the institution states that "The College of Wooster is an independent residential liberal arts college offering a rigorous and comprehensive education to students with the capacity and motivation to become educated leaders in a complex society." Enrolling more than 1,800 students and employing more than 145 full-time equivalent faculty, the student to faculty ratio at Wooster is 12:1.

Union University

"Union University is an academic community, affiliated with the Tennessee Baptist Convention, equipping persons to think Christianly and serve faithfully in ways consistent with its core values of being Christ-centered, people-focused, excellence-driven, and future-directed." Located in Jackson, Tennessee, Union enrolls 2,800 undergraduate and graduate students and has 230 full-time equivalent faculty. The student to faculty ratio at Union is 12:1.

University of Dayton

Located in Dayton, Ohio, the University of Dayton is "one of the nation's ten largest Catholic universities and Ohio's largest private university, with an enrollment of more than 10,000 students, including more than 6,500 full-time undergraduates." Founded in 1850 by the Society of Mary, the university states its mission to be "a comprehensive Catholic university, a diverse community committed, in the Marianist tradition, to educating the whole person and to linking learning and scholarship with leadership and service." The university offers baccalaureate, master's, and doctoral degrees and employs more than 400 full-time faculty. The student to faculty ratio at the University of Dayton is 14:1.

Villanova University

Villanova University is a comprehensive Roman Catholic institution that welcomes students of all faiths and was founded in 1842 by the friars of the Order of St. Augustine. Located in Villanova, Pennsylvania, the campus is approximately 12 miles west of Philadelphia. Enrolling more than 6,000 undergraduates and employing more than 500 full-time faculty, Villanova's student to faculty ratio is 13:1. In addition, Villanova also offers master's and doctoral programs in law, nursing, and other traditional disciplines.

Whitworth College

Whitworth College, founded in 1890, is a private, residential, liberal arts college affiliated with the Presbyterian Church. Located in Spokane, Washington, Whitworth's mission is "to provide its diverse student body an education of the mind and heart, equipping its graduates to honor God, follow Christ, and serve humanity." Whitworth's web site states that this mission is carried out "by a community of Christian scholars committed to excellent teaching and the integration of faith and learning." Enrolling more than 2,000 undergraduate and graduate students, Whitworth has a 14:1 student to faculty ratio with its 119 full-time faculty members.

Summary

The relevance of Personal Investment Theory to our study and in writing this book is twofold. First, we stress the centrality of meaning in human development—a sense of self and purpose in life, which can also be noted as vocation. Such a view is important to understanding behavior and what students do in college and later in life. We argue that colleges need to nurture the interior life of students—the heart and head—if they are to be effective in transforming student lives and preparing them for productive, useful, and meaningful lives.

Second, Personal Investment Theory emphasizes the sociocultural environment, which we have defined and described in terms of the 4Cs. Students behave, in part, based on their sense of self, but always within a context. We emphasize how colleges, through their programs, policies, and practices, enhance holistic student development. We also focus on how colleges invest their resources—particularly the faculty—in fostering student development.

The 4C framework serves as a way to organize the next four chapters of this book. Each chapter covers one of the 4Cs—culture, curriculum, cocurriculum, and community—as a way to delve into a more detailed description and analysis of what needs to take place on college campuses to foster holistic student development. Each of these chapters provides an overview of the findings for each "C," followed by different areas for consideration. The "C" chapters also contain profiles of the colleges we visited to highlight and provide descriptions of particular initiatives. Each chapter ends with a set of questions for campus leaders to consider. In Chapter 7, we step back to take a macro view and chart the next steps to help campus leaders become better informed about their engagement in the admittedly difficult but exciting work of developing students holistically.

Endnote

1) We use an inclusive definition of *faith* in this book, one that focuses on the psychological dimension of faith. Dykstra (1999) points out that faith and meaning are not identical terms. He writes,

> meaning, value, direction in life can never be the main points in the life of faith. . . . Faith involves transformation in life in which we hunger for a life in God or higher power, and meaning and value are likely benefits of our faith, but not the source of our seeking and hunger in our lives. (p. 30)

Thus, persons who consider the content to be essential in defining faith will regard this definition as limiting to their understanding and experience of faith.

3 Culture

"Who we bring in—students, staff, an
—Pres

"It is important to know that people
closed doors. The norm is being very
—Faculty men ... of Dayton

Introduction

The first C in the 4C framework is culture. *Culture* is a word often used to capture the shared values, character, mission, and identity of an organization or group of people (Tisdell, 2003). In the context of higher education, culture is used to describe the

> collective, mutually shaping patterns of norms, values, practices, beliefs, and assumptions which guide the behavior of individuals and groups and provide a frame of reference within which to interpret the meaning of events and actions on and off the campus. (Kuh, 1993, p. 2)

Stated another way, culture describes the ethos of a campus. It also includes vision—the intended future of a college, creating and sustaining a campus environment to meet its desired goals as well as the social norms and the accepted ways of doing daily business on campus. To be clear, we utilize culture as one of the 4Cs because we contend that campus culture has a direct, significant, and continuous impact on an institution's commitment to and nurturing of holistic student development.

In this chapter we present our findings on culture in four sections. First, we start with the importance of mission and leadership of an institution, particularly how it encompasses the legacy of the

…d how it is communicated. We examine how leadership …otes the institution's mission and builds intentional communi-…s. This includes ways in which colleges use vision in mobilizing the community to pursue their goals wrapped around their core identity and mission. Second, we note the influence that college location and campus facilities play in defining campus culture. Third, we examine the impact that faculty members have in defining culture, by their contributions and how they are developed and evaluated. Finally, we introduce the creative tensions between support and challenge that typify the campus cultures of the institutions that we studied.

Discerning and Acting on Institutional Mission

A college's mission provides a sense of direction, giving it purpose for being and doing. The mission is to be used "as describing its future, where a college wishes to go, what it wants to become or the impact it wants to have on students" (DeJong, 1992, p. 26). It guides the future growth and development of a college or university; mission uncovers the desired ends of an institution. The college's mission statement helps faculty, administrators, and students understand what the institution is trying to accomplish and "can be based on religious, ideological, or philosophical beliefs about human potential, teaching and learning" (Kuh, Schuh, Whitt, & Associates, 1991, p. 41).

The campuses we visited are unique in many ways, but they all display a strong sense of institutional mission. Mission at these campuses is not contrived. It reflects what Kuh et al. (2005) refer to as a "living mission and a lived educational philosophy" (p. 62). Institutional mission serves as the starting point for building a vision and plans for the future. The institutions in our study ask questions like—Why do we exist today and desire to do so in the future? What makes us unique and distinctive? Are we simply a "wannabe"?

More specifically, all of these colleges are committed to developing their students holistically. They feel that their mission is to assist students to know themselves—who they are and their purpose in life—to be self-aware in this global life; to develop their intellectual abilities; to cultivate social, civic, and moral responsibilities; and to examine faith claims. In other words, holistic student learning and development are both reflected in the college's mission and are taken seriously.

Many institutions have used strategic planning to discern their future direction, such as Creighton University, Pacific Lutheran University, Hamline University, and Union University. In doing so, they have taken the opportunity to reestablish the centrality of mission for their institutions. These colleges have continuous, deliberate communication through special programs, conferences, and roundtables for faculty, staff, and students that keep their mission and identity on the front burner, as well as inform those who are new to the institution. For example, at the University of Dayton, the institution is intentional in providing funds to support initiatives that meet its mission. The new strategic plan, called "A Vision of Excellence," was developed over the past few years to affirm its identity as a Marianist institution. Its accompanying document, "Focusing the Vision for 2010," offers a set of goals for the University of Dayton to achieve in the first decade of the 21st century. The provost has begun several campus-wide programs to signify this new era.

Another example where campuses are deliberate in terms of mission is developing and implementing offices of mission. One such office is at Villanova University. The Office for Mission Effectiveness was established in 2000 to promote and stress Villanova's commitment to living out its mission in every way in the Villanova community, to promote the Augustinian intellectual and moral legacy, and to support programs and research that reinforce the Augustinian mission.

The mission of Creighton University also has been the driving force behind its strategic planning process. This process is highlighted for the College of Arts and Sciences in the profile below.

Profile

Creighton University

In 2004–2005, the Faculty Senate of the College of Arts and Sciences at Creighton University formally adopted an "Identity Statement." In this statement they characterize the college using the concept of vocation. It "conceives of three basic, related divisions of our vocations as faculty, staff, and students of a Catholic and Jesuit University: Priority of Person, Nurturing Peers, and Affirming Faith." The college has labored throughout the 2004–2005 academic year to develop a strategic plan and to make the Identity Statement a living document. In doing so they have developed it within the vision for Creighton University "to be one of the top five faith-based master's comprehensive universities in the United States and the Jesuit school of choice in the region" (as stated by the president). The College of Arts and Sciences "will be at the center of this willed future."

They have identified four strategic issues and initiatives:

- Engaging the Catholic and Jesuit intellectual traditions
- Fostering an optimal community of inquiry
- Embodying *cura personalis* in the college communities
- Providing effective structures to enhance leadership

In this plan, faculty leaders told us about the energy and commitment to the college this exercise has created. As one faculty member in the Department of Theology stated, "Having a religious identity is not incompatible with intellectual rigor. Our distinction is our intellectual traditions. We want to contribute as a college and institution through our uniqueness."

Building on a Legacy

Institutions also possess a historical identity, or legacy. “A college’s legacy reflects its history, what it has attempted to be over the years and what it has become in the present” (DeJong, 1992, p. 26). It includes customs, rituals, and traditions from ethnic and religious backgrounds and from its geographical location. Legacy influences the culture of an institution. Many institutions have recently asked what their legacy is as they try to chart a course for the future. Others adopt an attitude of “if what we were doesn’t work, we can change.”

Of the colleges we visited, even though they varied in the extent to which they are consciously building on their historic roots—having “rootedness”—most of them felt more responsible for preserving the ideals of the academy rather than conforming to the whims and wishes of society. These colleges still adhere to the notion that an academy is most properly a place to form students and to critique society. Moreover, they demonstrate a sensitivity to the inexorable pressure to become too responsive and to yield too quickly to materialism and other pressures exerted by the larger society. All of the colleges have raised an issue identified by Mark Schwehn (1993), a leading authority on church-related colleges, that the “ownership” (p. 209) of ideas, curriculum, and education has moved too far away from the academy.

It is important to note that the denominational distinction seems to be waning at many of the colleges due to a variety of factors. At Catholic colleges, it is the decline in the number of “religious” (priests and sisters) on campus. The secularization of society has had an impact on the colleges in the study (Benne, 2001; Hatch, 2005; Marsden, 1994). At many Protestant colleges, a major factor is that the historical distinctions due to a church are being replaced by an emphasis on Christian commitment, which is more salient in the life of a person than any cultural or religious social patterns based on religious practices more prominent in the past (Simon et al., 2003). The great divide is no longer among church denominations, but rather between those who prefer a liberal or an evangelical perspective.

The colleges in our project varied significantly in building on a past legacy or building a new legacy. Some institutions have a very clear history or legacy, while others are circling back to their historical roots because they now understand their distinctiveness in terms of "where we came from." Moreover, all of these colleges are aware of their historic religious traditions, but they build on them in a number of different ways. That is, the importance of a historic church or religious identity varies among higher education institutions by denomination—and within the colleges of a particular denomination. In our study, for example, Union University has strong ties with the Southern Baptist Convention. The College of Wooster still maintains an affiliation with the Presbyterian Church (USA), but it has become more "service-oriented," moving away from the traditional "church-oriented" institution of several decades ago.

Institutions like Hope College, Union University, Villanova University, University of Dayton, and Creighton University are very intentional in incorporating historic religious and ecclesial perspectives into their academic programs (i.e., core curriculum/general education requirements) and into the total campus environment, and in conveying their core missions to external communities. For example, at the University of Dayton, the former provost plays a vital role in keeping the Catholic intellectual tradition alive, visible, and understood on campus through interdisciplinary seminars and workshops on hiring new faculty. Bethune-Cookman College is highlighted in the following profile for building on its distinct legacy as a historically black college and a college committed to its Methodist roots. These colleges recognize that they can and desire to be tied to their identity and tradition, appreciating and defending the liberal arts as one important way to identify their distinctiveness.

Profile

Bethune-Cookman College

In 2004, Bethune-Cookman College celebrated its century of service to the African-American community by renewing its dedication and commitment to its founder, Dr. Mary McLeod Bethune. Bethune-Cookman has few equals in retaining and building on its legacy, resting solely and appropriately on the life of Dr. Mary Bethune, who established the college in Daytona Beach, Florida. Its beginning was dramatic as Dr. Bethune began a college with "five little girls, $1.50, and faith in God." This woman, a daughter of slaves and herself one as well, had a spirit, determination, and courage to begin a school for girls that later grew into a secondary school, and in 1947 merged with Cookman Institute to become a college now affiliated with the United Methodist Church and recognized as a Historically Black College or University.

Her presence still is evident on campus. Mentioned by all with pride as a symbolic place for her legacy, her grave is located on the former city dump, which later became the campus and is now known as "Holy Ground." On her tombstone are the words, "She has given her best, that others may live a more abundant life," which is adjacent to the memorial home that she lived in during and after her tenure as president. Students, guests, and young people from the community visit this home to learn of her close personal relationships with President Franklin D. Roosevelt and his wife, Eleanor, and to learn of her role in 1935 as the organizer of the National Council of Negro Women. In 2005, a statue of Dr. Bethune was dedicated at one campus entrance. The current president, who began her tenure in 2005, has established a new tag line on all publications, "Sustaining a legacy of faith, scholarship, and service," that complements the existing motto, repeated by everyone on campus: "Enter to learn, depart to serve."

All members talk of the college's current mission as "tied to Dr. Bethune, its history, and the struggle in educating the Black youth in her day, and that is what we do here today as well." The faculty members talk of freshmen needing to read about Dr. Bethune (which they do the first week of a required freshman seminar course) with the expectation that "they live up to the legacy she has left."

Ceremonies and rituals reinforce the college's legacy. Each year, the president "swears" in the students at the local Methodist church on Saturday night to welcome them to a year of learning. All light a candle to symbolize the learning that will take place. At graduation, they have a senior consecration service that all seniors, parents, faculty, and staff attend. During this service, seniors again light a candle, this time to symbolize their commitment to serving others as a "Wildcat," their mascot name. It is described as "a moving, inspirational service" for everyone. Both events help to escalate kinship with the institution and its legacy.

At some colleges in our study, the link to a church denomination may be present, but the campus culture can be better described in terms of its evangelical Christian nature than its specific denominational affiliation. For example, students at Whitworth College are more apt to talk of being at a "Christian" rather than at a "Presbyterian" college. Four institutions of the Reformed tradition—The College of Wooster, Hope College, Pacific Lutheran University, and Whitworth College—differ in their reliance on their traditions to form their current identity. In recent decades, Hope College has reestablished a stronger identity with the Reformed tradition (Kennedy & Simon, 2005), although the students, according to the faculty, represent an increasingly evangelical perspective. Whitworth College has consciously tried to blend the Reformed traditions with an evangelical perspective throughout the college, including the faculty and staff as well as the students. With its emphasis on an evangelical perspective, Whitworth has conversations among the faculty and administration about its identity and character that are often similar to those at Union University, a member of the Southern Baptist Convention, which desires to embrace the Reformed tradition in many ways. Leaders and faculty at Hamline University and Bethune-Cookman College respect the liberal and progressive ideas and positions on social justice of John Wesley. But Bethune-Cookman has a culture that deeply reflects its mission as a Historically Black College and University. For Hamline, Wesley's views are imbued in its undergraduate curriculum, specifically its social justice major and the university-wide Conflict Studies Program.

Three universities we visited—Creighton University, of the Jesuit order; Villanova University, of the Augustinian order; and the University of Dayton, of the Marianist Order—are Roman Catholic and thus share much in common, often using the word *charism* to denote their special characters and identities. (*Charism* is a word frequently used at Catholic institutions to emphasize that the college consciously creates a distinctive identity and character to reflect its sponsoring religious body within the Catholic framework.) They honor and promote the Catholic intellectual tradition and are proud of the centuries-old support for education and the life of the mind. All have required courses in theology and religion in their core. All focus on experience, reflection, and action as a pedagogical approach. Catholic social thought is salient in their curricular offerings and permeates their programs. All three campuses have extensive volunteer programs, with an impressive number of students engaged in community service without academic credit. They all have had clerics as important members of the university community, and at all three institutions, priests of their orders serve as president.

Differences do exist on campus, especially in its ethos, as reflected in its social patterns and style. Those who have worked at Jesuit colleges and now at either of the other two consistently commented on the differing approaches to life and the structure of the academy. The Jesuits are more independent, individualistic, favoring argumentation, whereas a focus on community is more often the goal at the other two. Yet at Creighton University, they often talked of their friendliness and sense of community, partly reflecting the distinctive "plains and Midwestern" imprint on its ethos. All have a deep commitment to social justice, with the Jesuits especially of late (e.g., Kolvenbach, 2001) stressing it as a major pillar of their theology and way of life. The social scene at all three includes food and drink, which can be a double-edged sword, according to campus leaders. The vibrant social life at the University of Dayton reflects its strong sense of openness and a welcoming community, not the traditional fraternal society exclusiveness.

Communicating Institutional Mission and Identity

The colleges in this study use a variety of strategies to communicate their mission and identity. Sometimes a planning or strategic planning report or document can be used to parlay the mission. For example, at Pacific Lutheran University (PLU), the 2010 Report was frequently mentioned. The collaborative nature of the planning process to develop the 2010 Report has impacted the campus community and their support of the vision espoused by the planning process. Students, faculty, and staff all talked about "thoughtful inquiry, service, leadership, and care" and the importance of the PLU community to embody and realize this vision. The community was also energized by a sense of opportunity to integrate the importance of place and the importance of being Lutheran. Faculty were clearly debating and trying to take advantage of what it means to be a Lutheran institution in the Pacific Northwest. Similarly, Hamline University faculty and staff often rely on the Hamline Plan, instituted in 1985, to describe the character of the liberal arts and goals of Hamline's undergraduate mission (Davenport, 2004). And when we posed questions about what it means to work and study at Union University, many of the responses were congruent with the newly revised and unanimously received mission statement.

We also found that these campuses spend considerable time forming their identity and communicating it to various stakeholders using an apparent phrase, slogan, or motto. It may be a quote from a significant person in the life of the campus, a catchy phrase used by the president, a slogan used in recruitment materials, or a phrase that catches on in the community because it has been used so often and seems to capture the quintessence of the community. Villanova has consistently used one theme in the last few years to communicate its mission and identity. "Transforming Minds and Hearts" has been the title of its institutional self-study, most recent capital campaign, and academic strategic plan. The university emphasizes the synergistic connection between the mind and the heart, consistent with the teaching of St. Augustine, which is that "We train our minds to serve the human concerns that our hearts have pointed to" (Johannes, 2004, p. 2).

During our campus visits, we were impressed by the pervasive use of key phrases as they were repeated by the president, administrators, staff, faculty, and students without any prompting. The following are examples of common phrases that point to institutional identity:

- Bethune-Cookman College: "Enter to learn, depart to serve."
- Creighton University: "We exist for students and for learning."
- Hamline University: "Connecting liberal arts to life's work."

- Hope College: "Reformed in tradition, but ecumenical in nature."
- Pacific Lutheran University: "We challenge and support our students."
- The College of Wooster: "Nationally recognized for changing student lives through an emphasis on independent learning—IS [independent studies] drives the culture—it is the bloodstream of what we all do."
- University of Dayton: "Living and learning in community."
- Union University: "Southern Baptist by tradition, evangelical by conviction."
- Villanova University: "Compassionate minds."
- Whitworth College: "An education of mind and heart."

While all the colleges claim to prepare young people to be transformers of society, they have both mission and market in mind as they plan, advertise, and implement their programs. They experience some tension between a traditional liberal arts college—the dominant common image—and the practical issues facing them and their students. Since most of the institutions have relatively low endowments per student, they rely heavily on student enrollment to balance their budgets. This need translates to an awareness of the desires of parents and students in regard to a college education and the needs of the local community. That is, many are now marketing their ability to provide preprofessional education to meet the demands and needs of the millennial students' postgraduate plans. Union University, for example, has adjusted its curriculum to provide students with greater opportunities for preprofessional education for immediate employment in a competitive market. Other campuses, like Bethune-Cookman College, have responded by expanding returning adult degree programs, and the University of Dayton is placing more emphasis on graduate and professional programs.

All of these institutions know their competition very well, and most know with whom they want to benchmark and with whom they are now being compared. Almost all have an "aspirational focus," as one faculty member called it. Colleges market their uniqueness, often focusing on the value-added dimension, which always includes the theme of investing holistically in students. But this investment means assisting students with their career plans as a part of their calling and vocation. They recognize that the majority of students enrolled at their colleges do not desire an "elite liberal arts college" education. They come to college with strong support from their parents to prepare for a career as well as for life. Thus the colleges see as their challenge to creatively build on the creative tension between making a living and living a life.

Leadership

A large part of mission is vision, or what might be called picturing the future. Who communicates this vision? Authors on leadership can provide a context for what we observed and learned. Max De Pree, a trustee of Hope College for many years and former chief executive officer of Herman Miller stated,

> Management has a lot to do with answers. But leadership is a function of questions. And the first question for a leader always is: "Who do we intend to be?" not "What are we going to do?" but "Who do we intend to be?"

Being rather than doing is the core theme.

Leaders at the institutions we visited recognize the challenge of enacting a vision that embodies the meaningfulness of being rather than doing. They desire to be institutions that foster holistic development as a matter of course, but striking a proper balance in shaping students' cognitive, personal, social, and faith development is anything but simple. Likewise, maintaining and nurturing their respective institutional identities while responding to internal and external pressures is a challenging, if not sometimes daunting, task. One provost stated succinctly, "I need to be the person who needs to put it all together and implement it [mission]."

To provide context and to give some theoretical interpretation to what we discovered about leadership at these colleges, we use a perspective of leadership whose core idea is "leadership is a relationship" (Kouzes & Posner, 2003, p. 2), a relationship between leaders and followers. In this framework, effective leaders model the way by setting an example based on their own sense of self, inspire a shared vision among those they lead, challenge the process by seeking out opportunities and taking risks, enable others to act through collaboration and sharing power, and encourage the heart by recognizing contributions of others and celebrating individual and collective accomplishments. In this view, personal development is leadership development, with each person learning how to use his or her gifts, being self-aware of his or her talents, taking advantage of opportunities, inspiring and motivating others to follow, and recognizing the efforts and contributions of others. At the colleges we studied, it was evident that many presidents are exemplary in their leadership, and by being so, they are able to uplift the entire community. As one faculty member stated, "The president has made all of us more effective persons—he believes in us and also serves as our model." These leaders are authentic in that they know themselves and have a set of core values, link their doing with their being, connect their convictions with their decisions, and strive toward a common goal, not just their personal goals and desires.

Presidents and academic leaders consider that one of their major responsibilities is to be the gatekeeper of the college's mission and identity. As one provost commented, "We—the President and I—are the gatekeepers." They personally are expected to show conviction so that others buy in to the mission and goals of the institution. Presidents know they often set the tone on campus by their actions and decisions. They are critical in maintaining or developing the college identity, especially regarding the saliency of religious traditions on campus.

Presidents communicate the future of the college in different ways, leading faculty and staff to know where the college is going. They accept the challenge that presenting a clear direction gives faculty and staff a sense of purpose, and inspires dedication to the institution and motivation to address difficult issues, such as the priority of teaching and research, integration of faith and learning, and contents of a core curriculum. Moreover, their efforts help make the mission transparent to the students, alumni, and board of trustees. At Union University, students, faculty, and staff repeatedly referred to the president's intellectual leadership, openness and accessibility, ease of articulating a vision, and ability to develop a sense of community. He has provided continuity that has resulted in a stronger and clearer vision each year. In his inaugural address, the president introduced a worldview about loving God with hearts and minds. In each subsequent convocation address, he has built on the theme of "being evangelical with conviction." In the past three years, he has also "cast a vision" for scholarship at the university for all faculty and students. A faculty member at Union commented, "This place is all about leadership. The President has the vision. He gave us a shot in the arm and has given us confidence for faculty to do it. We have seen people rising to the occasion."

Presidents and academic leaders continuously repeat the mission to others and take every possible opportunity—convocation, graduation, forums—to communicate internally and externally. Although faculty and staff may be closer to the students, they tell us that they are reluctant to be engaged in controversial work, such as assisting students in their faith development or other personal issues, unless the core administrative leadership of the college supports such engagement in holistic development. Presidents consider the opening convocations attended by parents and students to be important occasions for getting the message out.

We also found that presidents and other campus leaders know the importance of getting external funding to promote projects that can advance the mission of the college. These projects are important because they bring external validation to the institution, pride to the community that someone else considers them "worthy of support," and a sense that campus members have been successful in competing with their peers. Such funding is concrete evidence that something new can now be a reality, which can reinforce an institution's strengths and reenergize or enhance current programs. Many of these colleges are able to participate in the "Programs for the Theological Exploration of Vocation," funded by Lilly Endowment, Inc. Seven of the ten institutions have been awarded a grant of up to $2 million dollars to develop initiatives that "assist students in examining how faith commitments relate to vocational choices" and encourage students to "consider ministry as a possible vocation . . . [and to help] faculty and staff to teach and mentor students effectively in this arena" (Dykstra, 2003, p. 1). Through this program, these institutions have been able to think of new ways to create a college community that fosters holistic student development based on the concept of vocation.

Provosts and presidents are more than gatekeepers of institutional identity and legacy. They also set the tone for campus leadership by modeling scholarship. At one college, the president is a very active scholar and is therefore a model for faculty who are conducting research, writing scholarly journal articles and books, and teaching. He expects faculty to be scholars and has raised the expectations on campus. Equally important, he has also provided support in the form of reduced teaching loads and summer research grants to the faculty engaged in such pursuits.

To summarize, college leaders deliberately engage in being:

- Gatekeepers of the institution's mission and identity in numerous direct and symbolic ways
- Role models for faculty, staff, and students by being scholars and educators
- Consultative and open in their deliberations and actions
- Intentional and consistent in communicating the college's mission and identity through convocations and public events

College Location

The physical location of the campus is a salient factor in a college's culture. In the past, a campus was often described as set apart from the larger world, highlighting its walls and single gate of entry to "campus." But this was not the image that was conveyed in our interviews, even though all of these campuses would be considered residential by most standards. Instead, we learned about the sensitivity of location along several fronts. First, the immediate neighborhood is an important factor. Sometimes the location of the campus was in transition and had a deteriorating infrastructure, making the need to relate to it important for social and economic reasons. (See more on this discussion in Chapter 6.)

Second, since these colleges do not enroll students from a national population, the region and location influences the types of students who enroll, thereby reflecting the culture of the immediate region. This factor helps to create a unique identity. For example, at Creighton University one administrator stated, "Creighton is very much of the Plains. Students are from openly religious families . . . students have a strong faith background." At Pacific Lutheran University, we noted the importance of place as expressed in terms of being a Lutheran institution in the Pacific Northwest, instead of the Midwest, which has a stronger Lutheran tradition. Villanova University, located in eastern Pennsylvania, attracts students from families that reflect the Catholic traditions of large cities in the East, with most students coming from Catholic backgrounds.

The location also helps to determine how close faculty and staff live to the campus. At almost every institution, faculty wanted to be close to campus so they could get to work quickly and because the close proximity gave them more opportunities to interact with students. Many deliberately purchased their homes to be able to have students over for breakfast, dinner, or other social events; they wanted students to be a part of their "extended family," something the students greatly appreciated. Many students could easily remember when and what homes they had visited. At one campus where the local neighborhood became either too dangerous or too expensive for families to live, faculty had to move out and commute sometimes for an hour or longer. This situation has greatly impacted the social life on that campus. Long-time employees noted with sadness that faculty do not attend student musical and athletic events as often and want to advise students by email.

Campus Facilities

In addition to the location, the physical layout of a college helps to foster a culture of holistic student development. Some campuses have recently built new facilities with faculty-student interaction and engagement in mind. Many faculty offices at Hope College, The College of Wooster, and Union University are located close to labs or student carrels. For example, Union's new science facilities were designed so that faculty offices were in close proximity to student study carrels. As one faculty member told us, "This way we are available for questions, including questions of meaning and faith."

Hope's new science center is designed to encourage cross-disciplinary links for a number of science departments. The designs of many new facilities at these colleges reinforce the centrality of students and provide collaborative research opportunities between students and faculty. Faculty members are close at hand to answer questions or go to the cafeteria for lunch discussions with students.

The location and facilities of the residential housing at the University of Dayton is another illustration of an institutional culture committed to holistic student development. The University of Dayton is a comprehensive university that is highly residential—95 % of its 6,700 undergraduates live in residence halls on the core campus or within a clear geographical boundary designated by the university's master plan, which is recognized by the city and the community as the "campus area." The area contains three university residential neighborhoods that are adjacent to the core campus and are composed of single family homes and some apartment buildings, 80 % of which the university owns and manages as part of its residential system. The remaining 20 % of the properties are owned by private landlords who rent to university students. The result is a residential area surrounding the core campus that is composed exclusively of students, university residence staff, and small Marianist religious communities. The university intentionally assigns all first-year students to traditional-style residence halls located on the core area of the campus. Sophomores, juniors, and seniors compete for housing assignments through lotteries in which seniors get first choice of the highly prized university-owned houses in the south neighborhood (affectionately referred to by generations of students as the student "Ghetto"), the north neighborhood, and the "Holy Angels" neighborhood. These housing arrangements intentionally foster the special campus culture of community and family, which are defining characteristics of the Marianist approach to education.

Other physical facilities can also promote undergraduate and graduate interaction. The president at Creighton University spoke with pride about how the new science building connects the undergraduate science building with the medical school. There is a huge lounge that is filled everyday with freshmen intermingling with professional students. He argues, "The fact that undergraduate freshmen can talk to a third year medical student is not just role modeling for them, but also instructional and [involves] mentoring."

The physical environment of a campus can also present a challenge. For example, Creighton University has a long, thin corridor down the middle of its campus. Whether by design or by chance, all of the academic buildings are on one side of the mall, and all of the residence life buildings and the student center are on the other side. Although the mall is rather narrow, it can act as a "big dividing line." The provost acknowledged to us that they are trying to break down that line because "what happens in class is then replayed a thousand times in the dorms and the impact of what happens is that then the residence life side hits every classroom the next day!" They want all constituencies—faculty, administrators, and students—to know what is happening on their campus and to enhance student interaction with campus leaders.

Expectations and Contributions of Faculty

At the institutions we studied, their mission, legacy, leadership, facilities, and location are critical for establishing and maintaining a culture that puts holistic student development first. However, it is the faculty who are, in essence, the keepers of the culture. The heart of these institutions is the formation and development of students, and faculty play a key role inside and outside of the classroom. While one president can do much to set a campus in a particular direction and student affairs professionals do much to carry out campus missions, the faculty are responsible for maintaining and communicating a culture of holistic student development on a daily basis. When we talked to students about campus life, nearly all referred to the faculty as the most important part of their college experiences.

Faculty as Role Models

Part of being a faculty member is being a good role model, which, for the colleges and universities in this study, is part of the cultural expectation. The faculty we spoke with see themselves as role models and they like being respected as important adult figures in students' lives. When faculty were asked if they consciously view themselves as role models, one faculty member at Hamline University stated:

> Yes, students want to spend time with me, asking me often for my opinion. This is different from my generation of the 1960s when no one trusted anyone over 30. I am regarded as a surrogate mother. What do I do with this recognition? I need to reflect on a very practical level. I need to make changes in my own personal life—to become more congruent with my beliefs and my behavior—what I am and what I do. This all means that I need to do the little stuff that is ethical, like returning a phone call.

Another faculty member noted, "I see this as a call. I view my work in terms of ministry. It is a scary thing. But I like what Sharon Parks says, that there are many role models on campus." She reinforces Parks's (2000) argument for a mentoring community in which students develop by having many mentors. This idea of multiple mentors was stated beautifully by a professor at Whitworth College, who commented on his perspective of the community at his college: "The genius of Whitworth as a place to work and study is that there are more models than molds."

Faculty and academic leaders recognize that faculty are powerful models by how they behave. Everyone strongly supports the rule of "walking the talk," preferring to demonstrate their convictions and values by what they do and how they do it. As the provost of Hope College stated, "Our walk is one of the greatest testimonies." At The College of Wooster, one senior faculty member noted, "The faculty are not trained or told to put forth their religious lives, nor is it welcomed in the classroom. You don't need to talk—just model it."

Based on discussions with faculty and administrators, we offer the following suggestions and questions to reflect upon:

- *Know the official policies of the college.* Some colleges may have explicit expectations—what faculty should or should not say and do in the classroom or in interactions with students.
- *Know the culture, identity, and ethos of the campus.* What is the tradition of sharing among faculty, staff, and students? What are appropriate and inappropriate behaviors and actions?
- *Allow faculty to be themselves.* Some are more comfortable than others with sharing their values. Some prefer to let their actions and achievements do the talking.
- *Know the dangers and consequences of getting too close to students.* Can a faculty member handle a pastoral and counseling role? Are such roles appropriate for faculty?
- *Be aware of the confidentiality issues involved in knowing the personal lives of students.*
- *Identify who on campus are the professional and trustworthy referrals when a faculty or staff member concludes that a student should consider professional help.*

- *Schedule faculty development meetings so that faculty and academic leaders can share their perspectives and experiences.*
- *Develop formal programs that assist faculty in dealing with personal values in their teaching and research.*
- *Do not expect integration to be equally apparent and practiced in all disciplines.* Incorporating issues of faith and values development is often more possible in the humanities and some professional programs as compared to the sciences.

Using a Career Perspective on Faculty Development

Who determines the culture of a campus? Almost everyone noted the importance of the people—faculty, administrators, staff, and students—in defining and maintaining a culture. In other words, institutional fit among the mission and the faculty, administrators, staff, and students is very important to the campuses we studied. The president of Creighton University stated it succinctly: "Who we bring in—students, staff, and faculty—creates the culture." These institutions hire faculty who support the mission, and they provide faculty mentoring and development. These actions form intentional communities.

College leaders and faculty in the study stressed a lifelong perspective of faculty development, viewed as three interlocking stages: recruitment and selection, orientation and mentoring, and lifelong professional and personal development.

Recruitment and Selection

The notion of "fit" and "fitting in" with campus culture was a recurring theme in our visits. Institutions expect faculty to respect the tradition of the college and its mission. The theme of "fit" is clear. Faculty members need to fit into the relatively small campus communities, since others are counting on them to be trustworthy team members and players. "If a faculty member does not enjoy being close to students and fellow faculty members, this may not be the place for him or her," noted one provost. Faculty members are eventually expected to become leaders among their peers. In our conversations, we implicitly heard that faculty should demonstrate qualities of character such as integrity, perseverance, and courage as identified by Glassick, Huber, and Maeroff (1997): "Certain qualities associated with a scholar's character are recognized by virtually all higher education institutions as consequential not only for the individual professor but for the entire community of scholars" (p. 61).

At these colleges, faculty development begins before faculty arrive on campus. Selecting for fit is the first step, but some leaders are beginning to recognize that it is not the only step. Colleges who take the entire career life span into account are creating policies and programs to make development a career-long venture. To them it is much more than just hiring good people who will fit in. Faculty need to be nurtured within the college community. Leaders have begun to view faculty development without recruitment and recruitment without development as incomplete (Heft, Katsuyama, & Pestello, 2001). Faculty development properly begins with recruitment and continues throughout the life of the faculty member.

Hiring for fit is not a straightforward process of finding the perfect match, because colleges seek both continuity with tradition and the kind of diversity that can contribute to a rich educational experience for students. Sometimes difference is sought rather than more of the same. Colleges want faculty to do more than just fit in; they want them to support and challenge the existing culture and goals. As a faculty member at one college mentioned, "Since the applicant would fit in too well, we did not hire him." At Creighton University, a dean gave us this insight:

> I inform the chairs that I prefer to talk about readiness rather than fit. It is more a question of openness

> and readiness. If you only look at the people who already know the right answers, I think you are going to end up with some real restrictions.

This dean talked to us about the importance of potential hires having a disposition and yearning to come to campus. Since not all new faculty will be familiar with the history and traditions of a campus, he stresses that the prospective faculty member should be open to and supportive of the mission of the college, including the centrality of holistic student development for its efforts, but that is not all.

Some colleges intentionally hire faculty and staff who have a commitment to a faith tradition as well as excellent academic credentials. Hope College has a deliberate method of hiring in each department by asking prospective candidates about their convictions in regard to a liberal arts education and their faith tradition. The notion of "fitting in" at Union University was mentioned numerous times during the site visit. The institution intentionally hires faculty that are serious about Christian faith, have good academic credentials, and love to teach and invest in the lives of students. Prospective faculty candidates are required to state they are "professing Christians" and write about their conversion experience, personal faith, and philosophy of teaching.

In other institutions, the love to teach and invest in the lives of students is stressed while in others the ethos of excellent teaching and cutting-edge research is stressed. The president of The College of Wooster desires to attract and select faculty who put teaching undergraduate students first and foremost. He prefers that a candidate's interest in teaching and research be equal. If research is favored, the fit may not be a good one for the person and for the college. As he stated, "Faculty here need to have a passion for working with 18–21 year olds." One recent faculty member hired at The College of Wooster reflected the president's vision when he told us,

> I came [here] because I wanted to get to know students. I love the interaction with students. I selected this institution because of the physical facilities, personnel, and how people here get along with each other. I am happy here because I am making a meaningful contribution.

We offer the following principles based on the premise that an explicit and intentional method of hiring faculty can effectively highlight the importance of "fit" in the college community:

- *Become more explicit and upfront about who is hired.* As one provost stated, "We don't apologize for our mission and identity." This is achieved in a number of ways; one is asking faculty to write a statement of how they can contribute to the college. Creighton University has this request:

  > On a separate sheet, please write on the following: What you understand as the mission of a liberal-arts, church-related institution like Creighton University and how your discipline and your background would enhance it. Include a statement on your philosophy of teaching and the nature and extent of your commitment to teaching.

- *Adopt policies that foster diversity of faculty views,* even though many institutions start with some conditions and expectations involving faith and social interactions. At every college, administrators and faculty express a deep concern about becoming too homogeneous, creating a "clannish atmosphere." Those with a strong set of requirements thus struggle about whether they will get the strongest scholars to apply.

- *Discuss the practice that the president and the provost often assume the responsibility of being gatekeepers of the mission and legacy of the institution.* Recognize that compromises are sometimes needed if faculty promote the disciplinary skills of the person, and the provost and president defend the principle of faculty members fitting in, supporting, and shaping the mission and identity of the institution.

- *Treat the campus visit as essential,* with the president and/or provost possibly taking an active role in the hiring process. When interviewing for faculty positions, the president of The College of Wooster asks candidates this question: "Across all of your schooling, who is your favorite teacher and why?" In answering, the candidate identifies with someone who cares about others and helps students to grow and learn. He prefers applicants who mention their elementary school teacher rather than their Ph.D. advisor. At Pacific Lutheran University, the president examines the faculty candidate with an eye to "whether or not the applicant will be a good department chairperson in the future."

Orientation and Mentoring Programs

Orientation programs are commonly used to help faculty with the socialization process in the first years of their careers at the college. Such programs are intended to promote and foster faculty as lifelong contributing members of the community. Moreover, they strive to fulfill individual and institutional needs simultaneously. That is, faculty are able to develop their career goals and fulfill the mission of the institution. We often heard that it does not take long for faculty to know if they desire to stay at the college, and those who do not fit tend to leave quite early. Lack of fit may relate to the social environment and demands of the college community on their personal lives—demands to teach more than they desire—and colleagueship.

We repeatedly heard that new faculty often need assistance and support to "unlearn" many of the habits, perspectives, and even attitudes they bring to their campuses from their graduate education. Since most of the faculty receive their advanced training from public and private research universities with little or no religious or undergraduate focus (i.e., no strong commitment to the importance of holistic student development), faculty are ill equipped to meet the special challenges of working in a small undergraduate college that emphasizes quality of teaching and a strong cohesive community (Gaff, 2004). Faculty are greatly influenced by their graduate training, with about one in three faculty at religiously affiliated colleges regarding their graduate faculty advisors as "very influential" in shaping their careers (Lindholm, 2004, p. 635).

At most of the colleges in the study, mentoring faculty is often done informally, but it is growing in importance. Academic leaders value the legacy of the college, and it is important to pass it on to the next generations. "Mentoring links traditions with the future through helping the coming generation become its best self. Mentoring is the voice of experience" (Simon et al., 2003, pp. 18–19). At these colleges, mentoring is one practice that deliberately connects the new with the experienced to ensure the continuity of the legacy and salient values of the institution and foster holistic student development.

These institutions use a variety of faculty development strategies that reflect an investment in faculty. Many are intended to highlight the mission and identity of the colleges, which stress fostering holistic student development. Some strategies include:

- *Visits to local churches and social organizations to illustrate the community's commitment to social justice or religious traditions:* This includes tours of the local community, meetings with leaders to get acquainted with the local culture and the sociocultural opportunities, and lectures and discussions on the intellectual traditions of the church and college.

- *Presentations of the college's mission and identity:* Increasingly, new faculty are being educated on the mission and identity of the college. At Hope College, a retired and highly respected faculty member well versed in the tradition of the College and in a Reformed worldview, makes presentations to new faculty about the culture of the college, emphasizing the importance of its legacy.
- *Communications about characteristics of students attending the college:* Student affairs offices and institutional research offices provide profiles of students as a way to begin conversations about the types of students enrolled.
- *College-sponsored social events for faculty*, often referred to as "social mentoring" (Simon et al., 2003, p. 36): In Hamline University's yearlong orientation program, first-year faculty learn effective ways to negotiate the community and know the rules of interactions and policies. The program also provides social opportunities for faculty to get to know one another.

Lifelong Professional and Personal Development of Faculty

That "faculty live personal as well as professional lives" is a statement we heard on every campus. All recognize the challenges and tensions that come with integrating their personal and professional lives. An increasing number are also beginning to focus on personal development, such as finding one's vocation as a faculty member (e.g., Whitworth College). The pressure for faculty to advance their professional skills, such as leading discussions, applying technology, and the use of research methods, competes with their desire and the college's espoused desire for faculty to lead a balanced life and develop as a comprehensive person—much like what the college community desires of its students.

Systematic attention and follow-up given to faculty development varies by the colleges that we visited. The following are some noteworthy programs and suggestions:

- *One-on-one mentoring programs.* Some campuses have formal mentoring programs, but many are very informal. Some are intended for mentoring for mission. For example, at Creighton University, mentoring during the first year involves faculty who may not belong to the same department, or even the same school or college. Moreover, the mentor may not necessarily be a senior or older faculty member. A mentor gives as much safe space as possible so that faculty can experiment and make mistakes and not have early trial-and-error ventures held against them.
- *Formal programs on pedagogy and use of technology in teaching.* Formal programs on pedagogy range from information technology services, teaching, assessment techniques, and learning how to use the library. One topic that is receiving increased discussion is integrating one's values and faith perspective with learning. At Creighton University, some faculty are awarded competitive semester-long fellowships during which they reflect on how to integrate faith and learning into their teaching, receiving three-credit hours of release time from teaching to attend faith and learning workshops and to focus on practical applications to the classroom.
- *Informal programs such as book clubs and sack lunches.* These gatherings are viewed as highly effective. A number of books about vocation and broader issues of education at church colleges are now available (e.g., Migliazzo, 2002; Poe, 2004; Schmeltekopf & Vitanza, 2003). At Hamline University, faculty book clubs are funded by the vice president for academic affairs, who considers them the best way

to help faculty develop community and express their personal values and perspectives with colleagues. Creighton University offered a free book on the topic of vocation. More than 700 faculty accepted the offer, and 100 had meals together to discuss the book.

- *Programs that help faculty integrate learning and faith.* At Union University, colloquiums such as "Dead Theologians' Society" encourage scholarship and spiritual development. There are also faculty-only collegiums comprised of 12 faculty members and some outside scholars who explore and read together on certain topics. In addition, Union's Carl F. H. Henry Center for Christian Leadership sponsors national conferences for integrating faith and learning and publishes a moral leadership newsletter.

- *Designated Offices of Faculty Development.* Also known as Centers for Learning and Teaching, the title is important because it conveys the significance of faculty development in the holistic sense. Funding is also important because it can have considerable symbolic value. The Villanova Institute for Teaching and Learning offers a variety of services to faculty "from all disciplines who are interested in helping their students become more effective learners." They have grant programs that encourage faculty to design courses that foster and integrate "moral and ethical values" in their instructional strategies, relevance and impact of religion and faith on society, public policy, the human condition generally, and international and interdisciplinary studies. At Whitworth College, the Weyerhaeuser Center for Faith and Learning is highly involved in assisting faculty in their development, as the following profile indicates.

Profile

Whitworth College

During the summer, Whitworth College holds a three-week workshop for new faculty who have been at the college for one to three years. This workshop is jointly sponsored by the Office of Faculty Development and the Weyerhaeuser Center for Faith and Learning, which is "dedicated to being a catalyst for changing the lives of faculty, students, clergy, and laity by assisting them in better understanding how Christian faith and learning are integrated."

Before the workshop begins, faculty are expected to read in their own theological tradition (e.g., Calvinist, Wesleyan, Lutheran, Evangelical, Catholic). The major question guiding the workshop, led by senior faculty and administrators, is—What is my vocation (purpose) as a scholar-teacher at Whitworth? During the first week the faculty hear presentations and engage in group discussions on theological issues and the history and mission of Whitworth College. Participants learn about the college's distinctiveness and identity, which is grounded in being evangelical in the Reformed tradition. Faculty also begin to integrate their faith tradition with their scholarship and teaching. They work individually with senior scholars and mentors in outlining a section of one of their courses that addresses integration of faith and learning. They focus on the questions—What might pedagogy informed by faith look like? What might scholarship informed by faith look like? In the fourth week, they make a presentation to the other faculty and receive feedback on their plans. During the academic year, the group meets individually with the leaders of the sponsoring offices and in group settings to discuss their progress in integrating faith and learning and to better understand the faculty review process.

Based on our campus visits, we suggest that colleges consider the following values as they plan their mentoring and development programs:

- Creates collegiality
- Helps new faculty learn the college's administrative procedures
- Reinforces the legacy and character of the college
- Provides opportunities for older faculty to use their leadership talents
- Builds social capital and trust among faculty
- Reduces the threat of social isolationism among new faculty
- Helps faculty develop a sense of commitment to the college and its ideals
- Provides ways for faculty to learn and appreciate the significant symbols, traditions, and rituals of the college
- Garners social relationships among families of the faculty; enhances faculty ownership of the college's mission and identity
- Assists faculty to learn, practice, and improve professional skills (e.g., discussion skills, use of technology)
- Provides feedback to faculty about their effectiveness in their role as a scholar
- Provides opportunities for faculty to give and receive constructive criticism to colleagues

Faculty Evaluation as a Reflection of Culture

One key to investing in students by investing in faculty depends on how a campus evaluates its faculty. A college that seeks to simultaneously foster individual faculty development and fulfill the collective goals (mission) of the institution is more apt to recognize the tension that can exist between expectations for and of faculty (Braskamp & Ory, 1994) The colleges in this study instituted a number of pre-tenure assessment programs, and some had post-tenure programs. Annual reviews are common at these colleges, with goal setting for the next year an important piece of the process.

The faculty evaluation processes in place at the campuses we visited had a formative and developmental approach to faculty development and assessment. The Latin root of the word assessment is *assidere*, which means to "sit beside." The image of "sitting beside" as cornerstone of faculty assessment was prevalent. "Sitting beside" implies dialogue and discourse and understanding the other's perspective before making a judgment of quality and integrity. It encourages a human perspective, building collegiality, and feedback. "Sitting beside" is in contrast with "standing over," which portrays a detached, self-proclaimed neutrality and by implication and perception, a superiority (Braskamp & Ory, 1994). The process can be described as stressing high standards but not standardization (Braskamp, 2000).

The provosts and deans in the study talked about faculty work in terms of contributions and a faculty member's contribution to advancing the goals and mission of the institution, college/school, and department. Given the size of the colleges, the leaders spoke with pride about the unique contributions of some faculty to the mission, character, and identity of the local college community. They informally know of individual faculty's quality of teaching, outreach activities, advising, academic program development, participation in governance, mentoring of students and colleagues, collegiality, and leadership in advancing the institutional mission and goals in teaching, research, service, and engagement in the community. They could often identify those serving as effective role models in the community. At colleges stressing holistic education within the context of an explicit Christian mission, faculty who fostered students to integrate science and religion, searched for personal meaning and ultimate truth, and assisted students in developing their spirituality and faith are well known on campus. Almost everyone—faculty, administrators in student affairs and ministry—seemed to know which faculty were not only advancing their careers as faculty members, but also advancing the goals of the institution.

This perspective reflects the importance of evaluating faculty for merit and worth. Merit refers to "quality according to the standards of the discipline," and worth refers to the value of the individual's "benefit to the institution, the meeting of needs." Faculty can be judged on their meritorious contributions as determined by the guild of scholars in one's discipline or field and on the quality of the contributions of a faculty member to the local campus community; that is, their ability to contribute according to the local college expectations and standards (Scriven, 1978).

Two common questions are at least implied when the colleges mention their desire to determine the worth of a faculty member—Is he or she as a faculty member bringing value added to the community? Is the college a better place because the faculty member has decided to use his or her talents and energies at this college? Thus worth is defined within the context of the mission and identity of the college. Worth is imbedded in the relationship between the college and each faculty member.

For many years, The College of Wooster has had a four-part "Criteria of Evaluation for Reappointments, Promotion, and Tenure." The four parts include:

- *Excellence in teaching is essential*

- *Scholarship*, which requires the faculty member to "remain abreast of new developments in one's discipline and may include efforts to expand one's intellectual interests beyond that discipline"
- *Research*, which is "defined as efforts to extend the bounds of knowledge and to share the results both with the professional community at large as well as with colleagues at Wooster in ways and forms appropriate to a given discipline"
- *General value to the college*

By explicitly including general value to the college community, the evaluation emphasizes the importance of worth. That is, faculty are expected to be active members of a "residential institution." Faculty are to be advisors, participate in the "intellectual and cultural life of the campus" and be good, contributing citizens. It was stated that "Wooster takes pride in the versatility of its faculty." Diversity is desired, as well as the distinctive and unique contributions by faculty.

The following profile of the faculty evaluation program at Villanova University is a prime example of how faculty evaluation and institutional culture are intertwined.

Profile

Villanova University

In fall 2004, the Office of the Vice President for Academic Affairs at Villanova University published the first issue of *Academics*. It presents Villanova's philosophy of education and how it fulfills its goals. In the Preface, the vice president highlights Villanova's identity with four words: "Transforming minds and hearts." To an Augustinian, the mind and heart are inseparable, and thus faculty are challenged to make contributions that fulfill this unique mission in American higher education. To fulfill its goals, Villanova has developed a new system of evaluating faculty. The new language used in the process, beginning in the 2003–2004 academic year, clearly communicates to the faculty the centrality of the Augustinian identity. The directive from the Office of the Academic Vice President is as follows: "Data regarding teaching, professional activities and intellectual contributions are needed to prepare faculty annual merit reviews and departmental end-of-year- reports. . . . Thank you for your many contributions to Villanova." The Office of Academic Affairs has added new requirements to the review, including the following items under the three major categories of teaching and academic counseling, research and publications, and service, respectively:

- List all teaching activities this year that integrate the values of the Augustinian tradition, Catholic school teaching, ethics, and social responsibility into your courses.
- Among the publications, paper presentations, and grant-seeking activities, indicate which ones specifically relate to advancing the values and mission of the college and university.
- Please list college or university activities that you have organized or participated in that advance the value and mission of the Augustinian tradition.

The fourth major category of the form, professional development, includes two questions:

- What steps are you planning to take to improve your performance as noted in the previous three sections?

- What additional resources, if any, do you need to enact these plans?

The colleges we studied have a distinctive philosophy and approach to faculty evaluation. The elements include the following:

- *Assessment reflects the image of "sitting beside" more than "standing over."* Faculty see assessment in terms of developing students and their peers. Some faculty talked in terms of a desire to "assess gracefully"; that is, to honor and uplift the personhood of students and peers in their judgments of their contributions. They often struggle with respecting the student as a person and holding them accountable for their actions and behavior. Being friends with colleagues complicates the judging process.

- *The mission of the college influences the standards of excellence.* The research-oriented institutions stressed more indicators of research productivity. Those with a strong teaching mission infrequently have a numerical minimum threshold of publications as an expectation.

- *Effective teaching and mentoring of faculty, along with colleagueship, are regarded as highly related forms of faculty leadership.* Being a good teacher carries considerable significance in the college community.

- *Merit and worth are valued, at least implicitly.* More and more colleges are developing explicit guidelines and standards that reflect all faculty contributions.

- *Quality is defined in terms of its transcendent nature and holistic character rather than in numbers.* Colleges prefer to engage in the fight against reductionism than accept highly behavioral measures of quality (Jacobsen & Jacobsen, 2004).

> They would agree with Robert Stake, a noted expert in measurement and assessment, that "so often we fail to see that the whole is greatly different from the sum of the parts. . . . There is a large market for the simple" (2004, p. 171).

Support and Challenge

The colleges in the study embody a culture marked by challenge and support as the twin contributors to holistic student development. This is evident in how faculty are evaluated, and it also marks the culture of student development. The colleges push and challenge students academically and personally, but do so within a context of support. The importance of balancing support and challenge in college is not new. First introduced by Sanford (1962, 1967), this concept has since been recognized as a foundation of good student development and learning. Holcomb and Nonneman (2004) state that a balance of support and challenge is needed: "Too much of either challenge or support effectively stunts development" (p. 102). For some time, colleges have tried to achieve learning and development by providing a new array of extracurricular programs in lieu of the classroom as the setting for such learning and development to occur.

In our site visits, staff and faculty mentioned the challenges of encouraging collaborations between two dominant subcultures—the faculty and professionals in student affairs and ministry—to integrate support and challenge. This dual role of support and challenge is especially relevant to the holistic development of students where the goals extend beyond cognitive and skill development into values, civic responsibility, and faith development. This culture represents a shift from faculty doing the challenging and student affairs professionals doing the supporting. Holistic student development requires both of these groups to support and challenge.

Most of the colleges we visited consciously address the tension of balancing challenge and support by creating collaborative arrangements intentionally. Pacific Lutheran University sees this dual responsibility of support and challenge as key to their identity, and thus includes it as part of their motto—"support and challenge." Faculty and staff there talk in terms of how they do both in their relationships with students.

Regardless of the differing views of the need to integrate support and challenge, everyone—faculty and student affairs professionals—agrees that developing students takes time and requires places for students to gather, discuss, reflect, learn, and receive feedback from more experienced adults. For example, students and campus leaders are aware that asking big questions in life that involve faith and meaning is not easy to do and cannot be solved by a set of rules and procedures. But it can be rewarding. One faculty member from Pacific Lutheran University captured the essence of new opportunities for faculty investing in students by remarking:

> Like student-faculty research and working with students on other projects, taking students to another country. . . . All the ways in which it's kind of "I can model." It's being that model of full intellectual life and life of personal integrity, but how can I do that alongside my students and allow them to work at this preprofessional level? And that's kind of given a new cast to all of this—I think that's fun!

Those in student affairs are often concerned that faculty do not see students holistically. A provost challenges her faculty to see both sides by saying,

> You—the faculty—have to be available to the students, outside of class. I don't think that means

> telling students what to do. But sometimes I think it means talking with students and reasoning through their options. . . . It means taking time, and in our world, sometimes we don't take the time.

Both academic and student affairs professionals expressed a desire to learn more about each other, their work expectations, and goals. Faculty members want student affairs professionals to keep them abreast of the most current research on student development theory and their experiential knowledge. Department chairs and faculty explain to student affairs professionals what faculty do, their constraints and challenges, and some of the influences on their work (including discipline, career stage, employment conditions, etc.). In short, leaders desire a cohesive community, recognizing that differing cultures and values within the community are also essential for an effective social environment to create a campus culture that is committed to holistic student development.

We often encountered the recognition that collaboration is needed and that more work is often necessary to make the campus a unified community. A culture of support and challenge epitomizes an institution's mission and identity, with the bottom line being holistic student development and learning. When support and challenge are closely connected, students are more apt to grow and develop, an important tenet of flow theory (Csikszentmihalyi, 1997). The institutions in this study are very aware that developing students holistically requires academic affairs and student affairs to work together. New positions, new centers, and new programs are being created that provide support to faculty to engage students more often. Educating faculty on student development issues is important as well. Leaders commented on how the climate of cooperation and collaboration on campus is a powerful factor in getting people to work together. At many of the campuses there is continual dedication to integrate these subcultures.

Summary

Colleges use mission to determine priorities and set the campus culture. The college's mission and identity have wide ownership and support. An effective education for students is not the sole responsibility of any one group but involves the whole campus community. The college's legacy influences total campus commitment to student development—intellectually, morally, and spiritually or religiously.

Putting students first is at the core of the mission and identity of each of these colleges. In their own unique ways, each institution is committed to developing students holistically. Strong leadership is critical to advancing the mission and identity of the college and integrating the colleges' subcultures—faculty, student affairs, and ministry. The following points help to summarize the findings in this chapter:

- Faculty and student affairs professionals expressed a desire to learn more about each other, their work expectations, and goals. Educating faculty on student development issues is important.

- Faculty development begins with recruiting and encompasses both personal and professional development throughout the careers of faculty and staff.

- A culture of support and challenge exists at these colleges. Academic and student affairs work together by creating new positions that report to the leaders and establishing new centers and programs that provide support to faculty and students.

- Special programs, especially externally funded initiatives, provide excellent opportunities for colleges to enhance a priority goal, create new administrative structures, and recommit to its mission.

- Students desire to have collegial relationships with "significant adults"—faculty and other professionals—on campus.

Questions for Campus Conversations

- *What is the mission of your institution? How does it reflect the legacy of your institution?*
- *What phrase, slogan, or motto does your institution use to communicate its character and identity to parents, alumni, students, and the community?*
- *How do college leaders at your institution take advantage of location and facilities to reinforce the college's identity and character?*
- *How does your institution's mission and identity influence the faculty selection and hiring process?*
- *How are faculty in your institution expected to guide students intellectually, socially, civically, physically, religiously, spiritually, and morally?*
- *How does your institution orient and develop faculty and staff to ensure the centrality of the campus's mission and vision in their work with colleagues and students?*
- *What kinds of faculty and staff evaluation are in place at your institution? How are faculty assessed for merit and worth?*
- *What evidence is there at your institution that it has created a culture of support and challenge?*

4 Curriculum

"We are not here to settle their [students] convictions, but to dig down—to find more satisfying roots. This is extremely difficult to do."

—Faculty member, Union University

"I will reveal my values only after the students have discussed the topic. The students inductively talk of their views. I do not want to foreclose the arguments."

—Faculty member, Hope College

"We like to know what faculty think, but we do not need to agree with them."

—Student, Hamline University

Introduction

The curriculum is the most important part of the sociocultural environment to assist students in meeting the college's desired learning and developmental goals. It represents "academic plans in action" (Stark & Lattuca, 1997, p. 7). In designing curriculum, faculty address a number of elements such as content, pedagogy, assessment strategies, monitoring, and changes in the curriculum instructional resources, evaluation strategies, and adjustments or changes in the plan (Stark & Lattuca, 1997). In most discussions of curriculum, student learning and development goals are also key elements in the design. These ends are often classified into content knowledge, skills, and attitudes (e.g., values, affect, predispositions). More specifically, the spectrum described in Chapter 1 represents the range of dimensions of holistic student development.

Academic plans are entrenched in the institutional mission and in larger societal contexts. Faculty members continually try to construct appropriate bridges between the past legacy and the future vision of the college. These discussions can become debates as faculty banter about the fundamentals of the curriculum. Levine (1998) has used the term *culture wars* to refer to these debates. Throughout the history of higher education, faculty have been engaged in culture wars over the curriculum, since it reflects the "centrality of the traditional canon in the undergraduate curriculum" and tries to address the "purpose, content, and meaning" of the undergraduate curriculum (Haworth & Conrad, 1995, p. 191). More recently, the concern over the curriculum focuses on how to educate students to be responsible citizens, with a moral compass or set of values. Katz (2005) argues that the academy may do well to reconsider the place of values in curriculum and to advocate a more humanist posture in undergraduate programs: "If we believe that values do have a role in education, then the challenge may be to rehistorize and rehumanize the undergraduate curriculum" (p. B6).

In this chapter, we first make a case that the curriculum—its design and implementation—is a fundamental component of a college's commitment to holistic student development. What is taught is the essence of the curriculum. Then we discuss the importance of pedagogy, since what and how students learn are interdependent. We focus on the use of first-year and senior-year experiences to integrate personal and faith development and learning into the classroom setting, and field-based and community-based learning (e.g., service-learning, January and May terms, study abroad). We present the challenges these colleges face in creating holistic learning and development environments, which rest on the ability of a college to create collaborative working arrangements among faculty and other professionals, as well as other "educators" from the communities beyond the college campus.

Philosophical Foundations of the Curriculum

How do you know what you know? For centuries the academy has been curious and mystified but engaged in endless debates about the basis and foundation of how we come to understand and learn what we know, believe, and are willing to live our lives by. The place to stand has never been universally accepted within the academy. For almost two centuries the work of the academy has been largely based on the philosophical roots of the Enlightenment, with its origin in the 18th century Age of Reason. It is based on the notion that truth is objective and exists outside human experience and can be known through value free, empirical, rational argument, and scientific methods. Scientific and empirical methods of knowing serve as the predominant bases for determining the trustworthiness of knowledge and understanding. This rationalist approach reflects a culture in the academy that relies almost exclusively on knowledge that is built on empirically based truth, critical analysis, and the power of science and technology in society.

Diminished confidence in the modernist perspective of the academy has immense implications for fostering holistic student development. Parks (2000) writes, "[If] the academy is dedicated to knowledge . . . [then] questions of meaning, morality, ultimacy, and faith—although very important—stand outside the realm of 'knowledge' and are beyond (or irrelevant to) the work of the academy" (p. 160). As a result, "commitment to the true has been divorced from the question of the good" (p. 159) in the academy. Where are, then, the issues of the "good life" to be addressed in college if issues of meaning and faith are not a part of the curriculum?

In the past few decades, faculty have begun to question and doubt the veracity and usefulness of empirically based knowledge to answer the questions of life (Wolfe, 2002). Voices within this counter-movement, often known as postmodernism, question the fairness and validity of what we know. In postmodernism, knowledge does not exist out there, but instead is a part of our being and is socially constructed; so-called absolute truth is not even possible, much less a goal. Knowing is relational and reflects one's culture and status in life. This counter-movement has made it possible for the voices of those representing the poor, disadvantaged, marginalized, and the discriminated against—including those embracing religious perspectives—to be heard more clearly and more often. It is this tacit inclusiveness that has given church-related colleges and the more exclusively minded, religiously oriented faculty a renewed status and acceptance in the larger academy.

As we learned in our study, however, some professors, especially those who teach at colleges characterized by an evangelical Christian ethos, do not agree with a postmodernist point of view on one important issue. Faculty who are informed by Christian faith acknowledge the influence of theistic and transcendent perspectives in the search for and interpretation of reality (i.e., the nature of the universe, personhood, justice, morality, and social interactions); they place value in a transcendent world that is the starting point for all else. The church-related colleges in our project represent a wide spectrum with regard to perspectives about theistic and transcendent truth. In addition, within each college, faculty members hold different perspectives on these issues as well.

Faculty members at the colleges we studied often said, "We do not tell students what to think, but how to think." However, faculty did not accept the premise that any position or perspective is equally good, useful, or valid. No one we interviewed argued for an extreme relativistic position. Rather, they stressed the importance of helping students to make commitments—taking a position, settling on a place to stand—while remaining open to change. They reinforced the arguments advocated by those who write about faith and moral development (Baxter Magolda & King, 2004; Parks, 2000). They also felt that faculty should take leadership in assisting students to understand and build their moral and civic responsibility around such virtues as honesty, fairness, and democracy (Colby, Ehrlich, Beaumont, & Stephens, 2003). In each case, we believe such approaches underscore the centrality of holistic student development at the institutions we studied.

Centrality of a Liberal Arts Education

The liberal arts are referred to simultaneously as a set of courses in particular areas (i.e., the arts, humanities, natural sciences, and social sciences) and an interdisciplinary core of classes that stretch student thinking and provide a foundation for learning. Church-related colleges historically have considered the liberal arts as the foundation of their curriculum. The colleges in our project have connected liberal education with the concept of vocation. Dykstra (2003) stated it this way:

> The word "vocation" also has profound religious connotations. *Chara* in Hebrew, *classis* in Greek, *vocare* in Latin: calling, calling from God. The religious connotations of the word point to broad terrains of meaning. They have to do with the shape and arc of one's whole life, with what one dedicates oneself to in every aspect of one's life, with one's deepest devotions, with who one most fundamentally is. And in this sense, vocation comes very close to what liberal education seeks for its students. In this sense, vocation may, in fact, be understood as the proper end or telos of a true liberal education. That, perhaps, is one of the deep reasons why so much liberal education in our history has been founded and sponsored under religious auspices (p. 1)

A liberal arts education is still apparent in the curriculum at each of the colleges we visited. Given the dual definition of the liberal arts—a series of classes and a means to liberate students thinking—it is not surprising that there are some disciplinary versus interdisciplinary tensions. While not all faculty have the same desires to contribute to the advancement of their disciplines as do faculty at research universities, where the pressure to publish is much stronger, many still define their professional identity in terms of their disciplines. Some faculty, but not all, practically regard the liberal arts as an interdisciplinary core of classes designed to provide students with a broad-based education. Some identify with the discipline, others with a liberal education in terms of thinking critically and creatively, and others identify with the college community.

The colleges in our study still have the liberal arts as the core of the undergraduate education. Even though a few of the colleges have graduate programs, the institutions, for the most part, are committed to anchoring their undergraduate programs in the liberal arts. They have not done what Katz (2005) states about research universities. At these colleges, faculty as scholars are committed to teaching undergraduates, and structurally, the undergraduate curriculum remains at the center of the college.

The colleges are examining their liberal arts curriculum and have adapted and conceptualized along several different fronts, each of which emphasizes the central importance of holistic student development. First, faculty view students as whole persons to be developed. They want students to develop a historical perspective and obtain a liberal education, and to be actively and competitively engaged in the world—to change the world while not conforming to it. To do so they work to equip students with the necessary knowledge, skills, and attitudes to change society from within rather than being isolated from it. They are willing to prepare students to be competitive with students from other colleges. They embrace the importance of a strong disciplinary education for their students.

Second, the colleges' curricula reflect their missions, which for most have historically emphasized preparing students for service professions (e.g., teaching, nursing, social work, and ministry) using a liberal arts foundation. The campuses in the study struggle to remain true to providing students with a strong liberal arts education while preparing them for the professions and graduate school.

Some, like Hamline University, deliberately promote and offer an applied liberal arts education (Association of American Colleges and Universities, 2002).

Third, they are responding to the needs of students and their parents with regard to expanded curricular offerings in professional fields (e.g., business, athletic training). The campuses in the study are responsive because they are student centered and keenly aware of the financial realities of their institutions and the need to offer a broad-based curriculum. They need to attract a sufficient number of students, knowing that an "elite liberal arts education" is not what their students and their parents desire. They recognize that preparation for a career is a part of preparation for life, not separate from it. Having a vocation—a calling and purpose in life—often is based on having a useful, productive, and meaningful career. It is both, not either/or, at these colleges.

Fourth, these colleges are trying to balance the traditional liberal arts (including theology and religions) in the core curriculum with student engagement in activities that develop students' civic, social, ethical, spiritual, and religious dimensions. They are adapting the curriculum to best prepare future leaders in an increasingly educated, pluralistic, and worldly wise society. As we note later in this chapter, many of the strategies called *engaged pedagogies* are now common on these campuses.

Fifth, college faculty appreciate the necessity of viewing the world from interdisciplinary and multidisciplinary perspectives, and, for some, incorporating spiritual and religious dimensions of life into courses (the senior seminar at Hope College profiled later in this chapter offers a good example).

Sixth, ethics and moral responsibility have begun to have a more prominent role in the curriculum. Incorporating ethics and moral responsibility into the curriculum is supported by faculty and alumni. For example, when asked what he thinks students remember most about the core curriculum (which is based on the liberal arts and Jesuit traditions), the president of Creighton University replied,

> When I go to alumni gatherings, students mention their ethics class. They hated going through it, but it has the staying power. We have retained fifteen hours of philosophy, religion, and ethics. In all of the professional schools, there are ethics courses, theoretical and applied.

Lastly, the liberal arts education at the colleges in the study prepares students to be good citizens and good workers, as well as good persons. Cantor and Schomberg (2003) refer to this as simultaneously being in the market (the world of work) and the monastery (a place to reflect on the larger purposes of life). While the phrase "earning a living is only part of living a life" still rings true to the hearts of faculty at these colleges, students—and their parents—are very intent on being prepared for a career and expect colleges to be responsive and responsible in providing an education that is useful.

Integrating Faith and Learning

The relationship of faith and learning has been a defining issue in determining the character and identity of all colleges and universities throughout the history of American higher education. Even today, the intellectual contributions of faith and religion—especially the perspective on seeking truth and what is worth knowing—have become more important in many church-related colleges (Benne, 2001). The anti-intellectualism once common in the "evangelical colleges" of several decades ago is far less apparent today. An intellectual search for understanding in this world—having a worldview perspective or an interpretation of reality—is strongly promoted at the colleges we visited. Central to this idea is the notion that autonomous human reasoning and understanding never fully explain ultimate truth. Those who advocate faith as central to understanding do not diminish the value of the intellect and reason, but argue that human reasoning without a faith perspective is insufficient for fully knowing and interpreting reality (Marsden, 2002).

The colleges in this study have a considerable stake in how they construct the learning and developmental environment for their students. It is reflected in their attempts to integrate faith and learning as one way that holistic student development can be pursued. For example, at Union University, all first-year students take an eight-week course in which they are involved in sessions titled "Discovering My Design," which focuses on God's design of each individual. The president of Union wants to see integration and scholarship in all of the programs and departments at the university, not just Christian studies. Faculty members introduce theological discussion into their small-size classes because they are committed to drawing out the implications—What meaning does faith have for you? What are the implications for carrying it out in your life? In class, according to one faculty member, it can be important to ask good questions that don't have answers, such as—Why does God allow pain and suffering? To him, the question is more important than the answer one may give. Another faculty member stated,

> We invite students to take a journey in our discipline and examine [secular] problems in society. For example, using practice methods of research methodology, I teach the art of listening, being slow to speak, and practicing the skills learned in a secular setting.

Another science faculty member said, "We teach chemistry so that students can do it and make sense of the science that they do—What does it mean to be human?"

But there are also tensions and challenges. In a group meeting, several Union University faculty commented on the challenges in guiding students to appreciate and understand the subject matter and the role of faith in learning. One faculty member asked, "How do we integrate faith in classes?" Another faculty member offered this perspective:

> As you prepare lesson plans, you ask yourself questions that need to be introduced in class. If you are teaching research, you involve questions on ethics—that's natural. If you are talking about death, you ask questions like: What is death to a Christian?

The faculty at these colleges have two goals in mind when they are teaching. First, they desire to uphold the goals and standards of the larger academy. They are members of a guild, often dictated by their association with their disciplines. Second, some faculty aim to critique, interpret, and comment, even provide, alternative perspectives to the dominant secular positions of the discipline. They desire to present alternative views based on their own perspectives and experiences or on the ethos of the college. A distinguished professor at Hope College describes his journey as a professor this way:

> I probably have changed, but I really don't know. I still think I am trying to do the same thing. I do teach differently. I do have more student engagement, more discussion, less lecture, let students explore, more emphasis on teaching writing. I am more student-centered. With regard to my faith orientation—same emphasis. My view of religion has opened up—I have learned how parochial I was from my own religious and theological background. So I try to get across a broader view of faith. When I teach at Hope, my

> guiding principle is to teach like I am at a university—cover the same things—the objective approach. The faith elements come in on their own—I am willing to talk about the religious dimensions of literature but only if they come out, not by trying to impose them. I never try to create or adopt a Christian approach to literature.

Worldviews

Today, the word *worldview* is a common and popular term to address the ultimate meaning of life. Each college has its own definition for worldview, but a good beginning is one a student gave us: "The lenses used for individuals to interpret reality." The concept of worldview seems to have several common characteristics: a human construct, a set of assumptions about the meaning of life, ways of seeking truth, and a perspective that guides the living of life. Faculty vary on their degree of certainty of how one knows what one knows and their propensity to be open to new truths and understandings. That the language of worldviews is prevalent on the campuses in the study is an indication that holistic student development is a primary focus.

Related to worldviews are the concepts of pluralism and diversity, topics that have received considerable attention throughout contemporary higher education. In general, the academy has supported pluralism, arguing that societies that are inclusive and provide access to all citizens regardless of cultural background, gender, and income are qualitatively better than societies that do not. Further, a pluralistic approach ostensibly offers a more enriched educational environment (Cantor & Schomberg, 2002; Zachman, 2003). Those with strong theological leanings, such as Wolterstorff (2002), argue:

> Allow, and even encourage, a plurality of voices: the Catholic, the Protestant, the Jewish, the Muslim, the humanist, the naturalist, all of them and more. Give faculty and students the freedom to let their comprehensive perspectives shape their work in whatever way seems to them appropriate, provided it satisfies the standards of the academy. It must be an engaged pluralism. That is to say: to be a member of the academy requires that one engage in the give and take of argumentation rather than each simply speaking his or her mind. (pp. 250–251)

At the colleges in this study, many faculty mentioned that they try to help students first understand that everyone has a set of assumptions—fundamental presumptions or a meta-narrative (i.e., worldview)—that interprets reality and the meaning of their lives. Then they try to help students examine the implications of their perspective. Faculty tell us that many students coming to college have not thought very deeply, or in a prolonged way, about the central perspectives they use to make sense of the world and their lives. In other interviews, faculty mentioned that many students come to campus with truth claims to which they hold tenaciously. These students see the world in black and white terms and view faith and learning as enemies rather than as friends (Perry, 1968). As one faculty member at an evangelical college noted, "Some students are afraid of knowledge." Faculty at all of the colleges generally agree that students today are more opinionated, open, and vocal about their views and thinking than students of decades ago. They now are willing to challenge faculty who try to challenge them to be open to multiple perspectives. Faculty told us that they try to emphasize worldview thinking as an important element of holistic student development. They guide students to embrace knowledge and move beyond dualistic views to understand multiple positions and ultimately define commitment to a particular position. Parks (2000) refers to the stage of many college students as one of probing commitment where students are experimenting and exploring a number of different value positions and commitments.

At some of the campuses, we found that the college community bases its curricular and cocurriular initiatives on its worldview. For example, at Union University, the new introductory core curriculum gateway courses emphasize the Christian worldview(s) as the central worldview(s), anchoring the curriculum and the co-curriculum. Faculty have written a book edited by the president and a philosophy professor entitled "Shaping a Christian Worldview."

At Whitworth College, the designed curriculum has a set of three core classes that emphasize the centrality of a broader worldview in understanding reality and one's place and purpose in the universe. At other institutions the religion or theology departments have the sole responsibility of articulating worldviews. For example, at Hamline University, one of the goals of the religion department is for students to reflect on their own worldviews. Through discussion and assignments students articulate their worldviews. The religion department faculty are "front and center" on getting students to learn how their worldviews affect their real lives. Faculty members want to get students to state a position, "since so much of our life is unexamined. Students need to examine what is too often taken for granted," as one faculty member shared.

Suggestions to Highlight Multiple Worldviews in the Curriculum

The colleges in the study vary significantly in how they highlight various worldviews within the curriculum, ranging from strong advocacy of one worldview, to consideration (although not necessarily acceptance) of many worldviews within an environment of pronounced openness. Some suggestions that we found for addressing the incorporation of worldviews into the curriculum as a means of enhancing holistic student development include the following:

- *Promote and celebrate pluralism on campus.* Faculty members have come to recognize that regardless of one's position on this topic, multiple perspectives do and should exist on campus among the faculty and students. At almost every college, faculty from different faith and religious traditions work side by side. They celebrate this diversity and see it as an opportunity for dialogue.

- *Defend pluralism on campus.* College presidents continuously defend the college's position on open inquiry in their dealings with the larger church, alumni, family, supporters, pastors, and students. With today's technology, students communicate easily and often with their parents and pastors. More than one faculty member told us that if he or she brings up a topic in a class, usually in religion or the social sciences, that seems counter to the teachings of the church as taught before students arrived at college, they call home immediately to their parents, who immediately call their pastor, who then quickly calls the president, who then turns to the provost who has the task of conferring with the professor. The president, who is the voice to the outside community, plays an important role in protecting the position that different voices need to be heard and debated, even though not all perspectives are to be considered equally valid and true.

- *Honor the dignity of personhood of all persons.* The search for truth must be open (i.e., academic freedom is a major tenet of the work conditions) and the personhood of faculty members and students as seekers of truth and knowledge must be honored.

- *Encourage everyone—faculty, student affairs, ministry, friends of the college, and fellow students—to be responsible for assisting students to develop holistically.* Since these colleges reinforce the centrality of holistic student development in the liberal arts curriculum, they believe student development should not be restricted to the life of the mind or the intellect. Student development is more than reasoning or learning; it requires nurturing of the heart and the mind.

Pedagogy

In recent years, the higher education community has begun to understand the connection between what and how faculty teach and what and how students learn. Given the emphasis on how students learn in college, the debates have begun to focus on the ways of knowing as much as on what students are to learn. It is important to the institutions in our study to link what is learned with how students learn. Such a view is consistent with the current national emphasis on student learning and cognition that challenges faculty to think differently about how they teach in light of how students learn (Donovan, Bransford, & Pellegrino, 1999). Palmer (1993) states, "conventional pedagogy persists because it conveys a view of reality that simplifies our lives" (p. 39). From what we could determine based on campus visits, faculty at the colleges in the study agree with Palmer that students learn more deeply and holistically by "interacting with the world, not by viewing it from afar" (p. 35).

Considerable discussion exists at these colleges about how to teach, as much as the debate about what to teach. Given an emphasis on holistic student development, the colleges in the study recognize the importance of creating safe classroom environments to foster student learning and development, and they are purposeful, from a pedagogical perspective, in how they integrate faith and learning to nurture holistic student development.

Creating Safe Environments

Faculty consider the safety of the classroom to be an absolute requirement. “The classroom is not a bully pulpit,” is what we heard from more than one faculty member. They want students to be able to share openly and not to be threatened. In some cases students said that the classroom was the safest place because they have a mature adult to monitor interactions. For students holding unpopular views on campus, they find faculty more willing to listen and to respect their individuality than their fellow students. For others, the fact that faculty have status and are the dispenser of grades leads students and faculty to readily acknowledge this important limitation of full disclosure. We repeatedly heard from provosts, student affairs administrators, faculty, and students themselves that they (students) are willing to air their faith and personal values only in environments where and when they feel safe. Given the importance of integrating faith and learning into the classrooms, creating classroom spaces that students deem safe is an important part of students’ holistic development.

Students vary in their willingness to share their personal views, some of it due to their backgrounds. Cultural and religious differences exist that shape the level of sharing religious, political, social, and/or economic views in public. For example, those of the Baptist tradition are more apt to share than those of the Reformed tradition, given the foundations of those perspectives. Students whom we spoke with talked about how they want to know the position of a faculty member in a particular course. If a faculty member talks about his or her worldview it is easier for students to do the same. Some students noted that faculty with more liberal views on social issues, religion, and matters of interest seem to get on the soapbox a little more often than faculty with conservative views. In all cases, students expect faculty to be able to create classroom environments that are open and respectful.

Fairness is also an important aspect of creating a safe classroom space. Faculty are intent on setting up classrooms in ways that encourage students to share their ideas and perspectives and to be able to debate, discuss, and argue their positions. Part of creating a fair classroom is setting standards for involvement that encourage students to share multiple perspectives even if these views are unpopular. A professor of religion at Hope College holds the following view, which is representative of faculty in this discipline at many of the colleges: "We are an academic community. We need to discuss and debate. We emphasize critical thinking in religion. Students want faculty to be more open about their views. How we frame a point of view is very important."

Establishing boundaries is an important part of creating safe classroom environments. Boundaries deal with when, how, and how much faculty share their views in class without requiring students to agree with their position (either implicitly or explicitly). Leaders feel it is important for faculty to be cognizant of their views and how they espouse them in class so as not to create an inappropriate tension for students. Faculty often mentioned that they recognize their power, and thus the need to establish boundaries and understand how the classroom is affected by the presentation of particular positions.

Faculty advocated teaching students how to think, but had different views on assisting students on what to think. Almost every faculty member we interviewed mentioned the importance of guiding students in their critical thinking skills. Faculty also mentioned the challenges of integrating faith and learning in the classroom. Expressing one's views in class is a personal matter to many faculty members. There was a fairly large range in how faculty approached the integration of faith and learning from a pedagogical perspective. Based on what we learned from students and faculty, many students are exposed to the integration of faith and learning as part of their college experience. However, the extent to which this occurs in any given class varies considerably. Some faculty are quite fluent in the integration of faith and learning and deliberately create classroom spaces for students to do the same, whereas other faculty talked about being open to having students integrate faith and learning (as long as it focused on class material) yet they do not do so themselves. One faculty member talked about her role as gatekeeper in the classroom to model civil and discipline-specific conversation.

Faculty mentioned the importance of dialogue and conversation and pedagogy that values student input. They have come to see the value of a student's personal and cultural perspective, with the person being a part of the learning process. Their goal is to have dialogue and conversations, rather than debate and argumentation, around class topics—to create hospitality (Bennett, 2003). A professor at Union University stated, "I try to create a climate and context for insight—where fascination is encouraged." To him, the focus is to expand the life of the mind and inquiry and have students think from a disciplinary and interdisciplinary perspective. Another young faculty member at the same institution told us, "We are not here to settle their [the students'] convictions, but to dig down—to find more satisfying roots. This is extremely difficult to do." Two things seem certain: to elicit convictions from students calls for safe and open classroom environments, and it is not an easy task.

Using Different Pedagogical Strategies to Foster Holistic Student Development

Faculty and academic leaders in higher education do not generally believe that a student (or any person for that matter) has the right to accept any and all positions as equally good, useful, or valid. Few students have this extreme relativistic position, and education leaders do not consider it to be intellectually or morally healthy (Nash, 2002). Likewise, Colby et al. (2003) argue that faculty should not only engage with students in values clarification, but they should assist students to understand and build their moral and civic responsibility around such virtues as honesty, fairness, and democracy. Those who write about faith and moral development (Baxter Magolda & King, 2004; Parks, 2000) stress the importance of making commitments in life—taking a position, settling on a place to stand—but they advocate that one needs to remain open to change and growth.

Faculty struggle with their own authority and expertise when teaching issues of what is true and good. Faculty mentioned to us the dilemma that Weisser (2005) has recently and candidly raised:

> When everyone is right and no one is wrong, what happens to the authority of expertise? . . . exchanging the intellectual authority of the professor for an ethos of self-expression among students is not equivalent to following the Socratic ideal of critical dialogue leading to self-development on the path to truth. (p. 29)

A number of trends have influenced the idea that all ideas are equally valid in the classroom, including

> the contemporary emphasis on self-esteem and the high valuation of feeling, anti-authoritarian movements and the combined effect of respect for individual feeling and the destabilization of objective knowledge as a liberating force for participatory democracy, student-centered pedagogy emphasizing the transfer of power and knowledge from teacher to learner, and television and other electronic media. (pp. 29–30)

To address this challenge, faculty employ several strategies of pedagogy to develop students holistically, assisting students to become more open and accepting of others and guiding them in their intellectual and faith journey of discerning what is true and good.

As a pedagogical strategy, some faculty share how they struggle with their own development to communicate that pursuing wholeness is a lifelong process. They illuminate how they use their "head and heart" to develop their values, faith, or worldviews. Some make a point of doing this without revealing their deepest personal feelings, faith, or values. They inform others how they try to integrate into their lives values and faith, to bring about an integrity and authenticity in their lives. They illustrate rather than persuade, keeping the process of open inquiry and reflection in mind rather than indoctrination. When comfortable and considered appropriate, faculty share their values, faith, and spirituality.

Faculty recognize that they are and can be powerful models. That is, do they walk the talk? They reflect the practice of their faith and values by what they do and how they do it.

A professor at Whitworth College, who has been teaching there for nearly two decades, stated that now he stirs up the class with a more liberal theological perspective, whereas years ago he advanced orthodoxy. At Union University, a professor stated,

> Students come in with a strong piety. When they get introduced to academic theology, it stirs them up. We want a cognitively complex person—wedding piety with theology. Christian intellectual grounding is needed to get students to establish their roots and find their position. In the 1980s, we destroyed students' faith—that is not true today.

Faculty in the study varied on how they thought about and taught particular worldviews. However, across the campuses, faculty were thoughtful in how they taught worldviews and how they encouraged students to establish worldviews relative to class content.

While faculty desire to influence students by their contributions, faculty also realize that students have views of the place and role of faculty in their lives. Some faculty are concerned about the nature of the relationships. One young faculty member gave us this image: "I am the vending machine and students put money in to purchase a commodity, which is me." Some faculty think that students assume they have earned the grade of B by simply being there, and others believe students see themselves as the customers who are always right. The students come to class and sit with arms folded as if to say, "Entertain me." One student leader remarked that his favorite teacher was "interesting and entertaining," and others remarked that "some faculty teach the subject matter but others teach the students." While they respect students as individual human beings, faculty do not view students as "customers or consumers" by and large. As one told us, "they are still students."

Thus, at times faculty struggle when deciding on the line between respecting a student as a person, and holding him or her accountable for actions as a student. How often do I need to give a student a break? When am I being too kind and considerate? Do I condone unacceptable behavior too long because the students are adults and I know them? Faculty and student interactions in the classroom (and out) are shaped by close relationships that develop as co-members of a community. These relationships in turn shape interactions in the classroom that in turn contribute to holistic student development. More than one faculty member talked of the importance of establishing boundaries in light of the close-knit interactions with students.

Generally, faculty members are not willing to accept the position that "we encourage all students to express their thoughts since there is no such a thing as a bad idea." While they realize that students prefer and need to be able to explore all things, they try to help students avoid relativism, where every thought, idea, and proposition is a personal one and thus worthy of equal consideration and validity.

Faculty and staff report that they increasingly encounter students who consider knowledge and truth to be highly personal, based mostly on feeling and personal perspectives, with insufficient intellectual reasoning and content. Faculty members at all the colleges—including the evangelical colleges—accept their roles of engaging students in a dialogue to address this reality and its possible consequence. Some faculty acquire a skepticism of logic, scientific evidence, and knowledge as a way to help students find meaning, while other faculty base their knowing on transcendent truth, using the Bible as an important authority. But at all colleges, faculty struggle with the search for truth, which keeps them intellectually vibrant and still desiring to hold on to the ideals of a liberal arts education.

The following are some common pedagogical strategies faculty employ to help students sort out their personal values, integrate faith and learning, and develop holistically in the classroom:

- *Conduct question and answer sessions in class.* Faculty members learn how to ask questions that guide students through an argument, separating facts from personal opinions.
- *Require position papers, essays, and written arguments of different worldviews.* One faculty member stated in the first paragraph that if a student simply states that he has rejected a worldview, he fails the student on the paper because he or she did not present an understanding of the worldview before presenting a judgment. To him, having a perspective is more than an emotional reaction.
- *Use books as references and authoritative sources (Bible, Koran) to illustrate how students can discern multiple views from books and writings.* Faculty talked about the usefulness of multiple resources to help students articulate and support an argument.

- *Play the role of devil's advocate in a class discussion.* One professor of history routinely presents counter-arguments. Some faculty require students to take sides and debate issues.
- *Use campus events.* Some colleges host events on campus as a way to connect classroom topics to current events. They take advantage of outside speakers and events, often planning them at opportune times to make connections with the classroom.
- *Personal journal assignments.* Faculty members vary on how public these students' perspectives ought to be. For some, only the professor sees the reflections; for others, students discuss their views in class or in small groups.
- *Small group discussions about a topic.* Some faculty use small groups to discuss class topics so students can deal more personally with class material.
- *Experiential and service-learning.* Faculty try to make connections between the classroom and the community to help students move out of the comfort of the classroom. These activities provide an opportunity for change and for students to develop and articulate their own positions or values on particular issues.
- *One-on-one sessions in the lab or studio.* Faculty commented on the value of these interactions, since they are frequently viewed as the most appropriate setting for more personal exchanges.

Developmentally Tailored Experiences for Students

The colleges in the study take seriously their role in helping students grow intellectually, socially, and spiritually. We often heard faculty talk about how they teach differently depending on the class level of the course. Intuitively they understand the intellectual and personal development of students even though they do not necessarily use the concepts that theorists of student development employ in describing the progression through college. Most of the colleges now have distinctive academic programs for first-year and senior-year students. Creighton University also has special programs for sophomores.

First-Year Experiences

The colleges in our study sponsor some type of first-year curricular experience as part of their core requirements. The experiences are designed to introduce students to the liberal arts and the learning process, and to begin the journey of holistic development. These practices reflect an "intense socialization" (Pascarella, Wolniak, Cruce, & Blaich, 2004, p. 70) of freshmen. The first-year experiences that we learned of have several common themes.

- Classes are small and highly interactive.
- Faculty from all disciplines and professionals from student affairs and ministry teach sections, using their own perspectives and experiences.
- The goal is for students to get to know faculty and professional staff members on a personal level during their first year of college.
- Discussion and sharing is a major pedagogical strategy.
- Getting students socialized into the college community is a major goal.
- Students are often required to read a common book before the start of their first semester.

- A theme for a required course is often a current social issue, a goal of a college education that reflects the campus mission, or a topic that spans several disciplines (e.g., "The Good Life," "The Environment").
- The focus is on first-year students beginning their journey of self-discovery by examining their gifts, their sense of self, and engaging in reflection and critical thinking in addition to acquiring a body of knowledge or set of skills.

The required freshman seminar at Bethune-Cookman College reflects an important and worthy Historically Black College and University characteristic—students are encouraged while in college to give back to society. Faculty, staff, and/or administrators from the college teach the seminar. Although some of its intent is to help socialize the incoming new students, the course is structured to clarify and renew student values. Students are asked to write journal entries about their feelings on social issues, such as election results, and their sense of self. The class sizes are kept under 15 students. After the first semester, students engage in a service-learning experience. Students need to devote a minimum number of hours to the community, with a focus on their culture. In the manual for the freshman seminar, the syllabus contains these words to highlight the commitment to leading the good life:

> Understanding and accepting a set of values will involve us in affirming the importance of human worth, dignity, and individual responsibility as we reach for knowledge, honesty, and tolerance. The broad goal of freshmen seminar is to learn how to function in this liberal arts educational community where enduring values should relate to lifelong goals. Another objective is to further our understanding and acceptance of a core of ethical standards that

"good" people use to govern their daily civil interactions.

The following profile highlights the first-year seminar at Hamline University.

Profile

Hamline University

At Hamline University, the first-year seminar is designed for students to get "personal attention" and "exceptional experiences." The seminar is taught by a faculty member who is assisted by a professional not on the faculty (e.g., a member of the Career Development Center or student affairs) and by a student leader. The staff member is considered a *campus colleague,* a term that has significant meaning to the faculty, staff, *and* students, while the student leader is part of the SOS (Students Orienting Students) team that develops the New Student Orientation Program. The classes of less than 20 students are taught collaboratively, with the faculty member serving as the student's academic advisor for the first and second year, or until the student declares a major.

Students immediately are asked to integrate their studies with their plans beyond college—to learn skills that would prepare them for a career of their choice and for life more generally. Students learn to construct a resume during their first years and learn and practice job interviewing. It is, however, "not just getting people into jobs," but assisting students to reflect on their gifts, their interests, skills, and life goals. Thus the goal is to encourage students to think in terms of a vocation or calling, the larger issues in life.

Senior-Year Experiences

The colleges we visited frequently have a special type of academic offering for seniors, often referred to as capstone experiences. These experiences are excellent curricular examples of the ways in which the colleges promote holistic student development. Common goals for the senior experiences include:

- To integrate knowledge and understanding
- To delineate the practice of particular worldviews in the real world
- To encourage reflection
- To apply knowledge to personal life

Every college in the study had some type of senior-year experience, although some are not required. The senior-year experience at Hope College is profiled next because it runs counter to the observation of Robert Wuthnow (2004) about the way religion and theology courses are generally taught today. He says,

> So is the idea that there should be a rather impenetrable firewall between however faith may be discussed in the classroom and however it may be practiced in one's personal life? In the classroom, the acceptable mode is to teach about religion, leaving the teaching of religion and the practice of faith to be promoted by chaplains, campus clergy, or student ministries.

Hope's senior seminar allows students to express their understanding of their faith in the course.

Profile

Hope College

Hope College's senior seminar is described in their catalog as "stressing personal assessment of one's education and life view" and is intended to serve as the capstone to students' education. The seminars are designed to help the student 1) consider how the Christian faith can inform a philosophy of living; 2) articulate his or her philosophy of living in a coherent, disciplined, yet personal way; and 3) provide an opportunity to understand secular contemporary values in a Christian perspective. Each seminar is built around a theme.

A professor of philosophy at Hope has developed her senior seminar course to examine the question—How good should the good life be? The course is titled "Saints, Heroes, and Ordinary People." Students read a number of biographies, novels, and stories that illustrate how various people have lived their lives, some Christian and some not, to "stimulate their thinking in pursuit of the three goals." Some of the texts include *Lest Innocent Blood Be Shed* (Hallie, 1979), *Ironweed* (Kennedy, 1979), and *The Killer Angels* (Shaara, 1987).

Students write six reaction papers to their readings and a short paper providing a statement of what students think is the essential content of Christian faith. This can be from a "believing stance" or a "distanced stance." Each student is "to display a college-level understanding of Christianity, whether or not the student personally believes it to be true." The seminar course emphasizes discussing and sharing among the class members, and each student is required to write a life view paper. Students are to "articulate a philosophy for living in a coherent, disciplined, yet personal way." The course's syllabus ends with: "Your life view paper should be yours. Please do it in a way that allows you to do your best at expressing yourself and grappling with the issues of the course and of your life." Students have options for writing about their religious perspectives and about their analyses of the readings.

Students are encouraged to use the following questions in writing their final paper:

- What is important enough to me to spend large parts of my life on?
- What criteria or guidelines will inform the important decisions I make in my life?
- Will I have specific long-term goals or will I just take life as it comes?
- If I have long-term goals, what will they be?
- What place will personal and family relationships have in my life?
- How important will work or profession be in my life?
- Will I work to live or live to work?
- How important will it be to me to help those in need?
- What will the moral principles be by which I act?
- What place, if any, will my religious beliefs have in my life?

In this class, the religion—Christianity—is not studied as an object, with students and faculty examining it as a scholarly exercise. Instead, they have an opportunity in a class setting to apply Christianity as a faith to guide and direct their lives.

Pedagogy of Engagement: Field-Based and Community-Based Learning

The pedagogy of engagement, usually in the form of field-based and community-based learning, needs a special type of learning environment, one that relies on the setting of the learning and the nature of the content and the desired student learning and development goals. Many of the institutions in our study use several variations of the pedagogy of engagement. They can be classified as:

- Service-learning
- Community-based service and research
- January and May terms
- Study abroad
- Student research opportunities

In this section we list the common strategies used at these colleges to foster holistic student development. We include here only credit courses and experiences. (In Chapter 5, we discuss the rationale and nature of cocurricular volunteer and community service programs, which are also very popular at these colleges.)

First, field-based and community-based programs involve education in an extended classroom, which means it starts with learning. Students give to the greater society for the common good, but it is done within the pedagogy of engaging students in real-life settings so they acquire needed skills and attitudes. Hands-on experiences are used as a conduit for learning, but they emphasize the heart as well as the head.

Second, this approach reflects a postmodern triumph over the detached objectivity often associated with modernism, as discussed earlier. This way of knowing relies on community experience for validation and the 1960s scholarship of protest and relativity. By the late 1990s, student research under the direction of faculty had blossomed on campuses across the country, including research on issues and problems in the community within reach of the campus. Increasingly, the colleges in our study are joining other institutions, developing school and community partnerships, and encouraging among faculty members what Clark (2000) called a spirit of collegial entrepreneurialism.

Third, it takes advantage of the personal and professional interests of faculty members, who often regard this type of involvement as fulfilling their desires and needs as well. This engagement is rewarding and reinforcing because it reflects an integrated life as a professor—connecting personal values and professional expertise (Braskamp & Wergin, 1998; Ward, 2003; Wergin, 2003). We heard from many faculty members who do not wish to separate their work from their life. Their careers are central to their living the good life.

Service-Learning

Service-learning is a pedagogical innovation that combines service and learning. Ehrlich (2005) argues that it fulfills three different functions: enhances academic learning, develops knowledge and skills for leadership, and fosters civic responsibility. Service-learning can achieve academic depth by extending the relevance of subject matter beyond the classroom and expectations of performance within it. Service-learning develops active concern for the social problems of the day within the context of academic rigor. Projects that involve students in direct service to others combine substantial processes of reflection and can help students understand the power of disciplinary and interdisciplinary ideas and methods. Students feel more confident about what they are learning because the subject matter comes to life (Eyler & Giles, 1999). Students receive direct social development benefits from their involvement while they provide social benefits to greater society. Many have documented that service-learning is relevant to the advancement of justice and democratic citizenship (Battistoni, 2002; Eyler & Giles, 1999; Heffner & Beversluis, 2002; Jacoby & Associates, 1996; Zlotkowski, 1998), both of which are intended goals of a holistic student development approach.

Heffner and Beversluis (2002) state, "Within the Christian community, service learning is about more than educating students for active citizenship; it is about preparing students to live a life of faith and modeling reciprocity between college and community" (p. xi). Reflection is a key element of service-learning, calling on students to connect what they are learning in the community with class objectives. Given their status as church-related colleges, the institutions in our study saw service-learning as an opportunity to connect service and learning, but with a particular faith perspective in mind. Service is not just about doing good; it's also a way to exercise one's faith.

The colleges stated common arguments for including service-learning experiences in the curriculum. These arguments include opportunities for students to:

- Experience firsthand the complexity and interrelatedness of society's social problems
- Relate theory and classroom studies with practice and real-life experience
- Connect with their personal lives
- Develop habits of the heart and mind
- Journal and reflect on experiences and then share them in class
- Develop a sense of civic responsibility
- Work as a member of a team to solve real-life problems

- Develop leadership skills
- Put into practice, under supervision, an understanding of the issues involved

At Bethune-Cookman College, all second-semester freshmen take a course that includes a service-learning component. Each student spends a number of hours in community service to fulfill the college's mission that giving back to society is part of being a human being. Bethune-Cookman was the only Historically Black College and University in the original group of colleges that was a member of Project Pericles (www.projectpericles.org), a national initiative that "encourages and facilitates commitments by colleges and universities to include education for social responsibility and participatory citizenship as an essential part of their educational programs, in and out of the classroom." In talking to faculty and administrators about this program, they often emphasized that service is couched in terms of a faithful and spiritual life.

Community-Based Service and Research

Community-based research is another form of engaged pedagogy. Students become involved in real-world settings, often in teams, to address societal issues and engage in problem solving. The problems usually require a cross-disciplinary perspective, and political and financial realities of these problems are part of the learning process. In some instances, these research experiences are embedded within the context of a service-learning course, and in others the community-based research experience is done independently with a particular faculty member.

Hamline University developed a major curricula strategy called LEAD—Leadership, Education, and Development—that was established in 1988 as part of the Hamline plan. It is "a broad-based experiential education program. . . . Designed to help students become leaders in a rapidly changing and complex world, LEAD reinforces and expands student learning by connecting classroom theory with experience." LEAD stresses the connections between the liberal arts and work. The brochure states that students will

> Make connections between theory and practice; deepen their understanding of the communities around them; explore their own values, interests, and abilities; increase their confidence in themselves; and develop skills for their roles as creative leaders and compassionate citizens of the world.

Students can get LEAD experience through internships, enrolling in LEAD classes where they conduct community-based research and service projects combined with reflection and analysis, and through "independent LEAD experiences." The internships, which can be local, national, and international, are for students who want out-of-classroom experiential learning experience where they can work in a local setting, attend classes abroad, and be in contact with a faculty member and/or consultant with the Career Development Center (CDC) about career opportunities. Administratively, the CDC is responsible for more than 3,000 internships available to students in the area and works closely with the faculty member who supervises students for course credit.

January and May Terms

Most of the colleges have a one-month academic program, which is in January or May. These terms provide students the opportunity to enroll for credit in an in-depth study of a topic, travel with faculty to an international site, or take an unusual course. Whitworth College sponsors a unique course, "Prejudice Across America," in which students participate with a faculty member in a cultural train excursion. This experience provides students the opportunity to be in contact with others who are different from themselves and to see firsthand the impact of social ills like poverty and discrimination throughout the country. Experiences such as this one provide significant exposure to the world, which ultimately prepares students to be better contributors to it. January and May term experiences are conducted, at least in part, in off-campus locations. But on some of the campuses, especially those in remote locations, faculty and students indicated that the collegiate experience can be isolating. Such experiences move students beyond the campus to new and different settings and put faculty members and students in close proximity to one another.

At Pacific Lutheran University, the collegial relationships among diverse groups on campus make a difference to students. The "J-Term" was mentioned by faculty, staff, and students as an important mechanism for providing specialized learning experiences, many of them in support of Pacific Lutheran's international focus, and, more importantly, the opportunity to develop meaningful and lasting relationships with fellow students, staff, and professors as part of the shared experience. When asked about the significant adults in their lives, students mentioned the lasting support of J-Term professors. The J-Term was also noted as an ideal educational experience to grapple with some of the bigger issues that students face (e.g., Why am I here? Where am I going?).

Study Abroad

Faculty and academic leaders are aware that they need to consciously and deliberately provide a diverse and pluralistic environment for their students. Historically, these colleges have a tradition of making connections with other countries, often through the church's related missionary alliances. The colleges in the study were unanimously interested in developing international connections and have many in place through their church denominations or through their associations (e.g., Jesuits' worldwide network of 132 universities).

Many colleges sponsor short terms (e.g., work and study camps) to foreign countries during spring break or during a January term to acquaint students with different cultures. These experiences foster intercultural sensitivity and awareness of others (Bennett, 1993). Often these excursions are couched within a missionary or service frame of reference—students are given an opportunity to live out their religious convictions by helping others and making a contribution to community needs. According to conversations we had with students and faculty, these international experiences have a profound impact on students, reinforcing the argument that students are more apt to be transformed through experiences and contact with people different from themselves than by reading about them in a class. In this way the heart and the head are affected (Kolvenbach, 2001). Some have summer programs that allow students to learn of the culture and provide assistance to the local host. These are often in the form of a work-study arrangement, reflecting and reinforcing the virtue of giving to others regardless of where the neighbor is located.

Some campus leaders refer to study abroad in terms of a *spiritual* experience. Living in a foreign culture provides a rich opportunity for students to better understand their own cultural backgrounds, values, and sense of self. Campus leaders promote and defend these experiences on the common argument and evidence that students consider the value added of their experiences in a different culture to be their personal development—increased self-confidence and knowing oneself better (Dwyer, 2004).

The rural settings and a distinctive religious or faith tradition of many of the campuses present an extra challenge in attracting students from diverse backgrounds. Sometimes the religious traditions that are prominent on campus also become a barrier to attracting students of color. Some colleges, particularly those with an evangelical mission, have deliberately recruited students from other nations to create pluralism and diversity on campus. For example, at Union University, the provost stated that they want students to have an intercultural experience, since an international experience is not feasible for everyone. By having as diverse a campus as possible through enrolling international students and aggressively recruiting students from all cultural backgrounds, they try to get their students to "face reality." Likewise, a senior faculty member at the University of Dayton suggested that church colleges can better achieve the goal of diversity by enrolling "Catholic" students from around the world, rather than trying to recruit a few minority students in the region.

Pacific Lutheran University is very committed to sending students to foreign countries to engage in classes with a service-learning focus and service projects. These programs reflect the university's goal of helping students become aware of the world around them. The International Partnership for Service Learning and Leadership, a third-party provider of students studying abroad, reported that two of every three students in their programs are enrolled in church-related colleges. These colleges are often small and not as wealthy as the elite colleges, but they are able to engage students through world and global missions and contacts, and they often desire to promote connections between being worldly wise and service to others (Nevin Brown, personal communication, February 1, 2005).

Student Research Opportunities

Boyer (1990b) argues that the academy must be engaged in the discovery of new knowledge and that faculty must be active participants in expanding knowledge. Across the board there was a press for faculty to be more involved in undergraduate research projects. Faculty are involved in critical analyses and syntheses of knowledge in many ways, and they regard research as more than producing reports of their creative and analytical work. Some viewed their role as more than critical thinkers finding fault with current theories and portrayals of reality and being skeptical of scientific knowledge. They wanted to create and construct knowledge as well as critique it. Many of the faculty, as scholars, view as their role to integrate and communicate results of inquiry, analysis, and synthesis to external audiences, including the general public. Faculty also regarded their scholarly talents through their performances in the visual and creative arts, such as composing and creating a work of art or performing a musical score.

The degree of involvement in research varied considerably across colleges and among faculty. Provosts and faculty often made a distinction between scholarship and being scholarly. Scholarship requires communication and public demonstration of the work of the scholar. In research, the product is clear (such as a written report in a journal), but in teaching, and to some extent engagement, it is the process—teaching, consulting, coaching, advising, and mentoring—that is the essence of being a scholar. Being a scholar—being involved in a scholarly activity—is not the same as scholarship, which refers to an outcome or product. Being is as important as doing for many faculty in defining their self-identity and contributing to their profession and college. Chief academic officers frequently mentioned the importance of faculty being scholarly in all their work, rather than only being producers of public scholarship. As one provost stated, "Faculty are to be model scholars in all they do." Much of the manifestation of the model scholar is observed in the close collaboration with undergraduate students on research projects.

Faculty members at most of the colleges in the project are expected to be good mentors and to be active in developing the creative and research skills of students. The College of Wooster is a prime example of faculty working with students on undergraduate research. The vice president of academic affairs and faculty at the college noted that although no quantitative benchmarks of research productivity exist, research is embedded in much of what faculty do. Wooster distinguishes between being scholars and doing research. The contributions of faculty are differentiated in terms of breadth and depth and how a faculty member can model being a scholar in both instances. Faculty need to be scholarly in advising students in the independent studies required of all seniors. They need to know the ethical and procedural matters of conducting scholarly work in an area, even though they may not be publishing or interacting with other colleagues on the research problem. On the other hand, faculty conducting research are expected to advance knowledge, which requires them to also be members of the larger academic community. The IS process at The College of Wooster is described in the following profile.

Profile

The College of Wooster

The College of Wooster is nationally recognized for its curricular independent study (IS) program that is more 50 years old. It is intended to change student lives through an emphasis on independent learning. The college requires that every graduate complete a significant project that provides personal meaning and is appropriate to their individual fields and interests. It has now been "integrated in the full fiber of the four-year experience," as is mentioned in the institution's mission statement. As one faculty member said, "IS drives the culture—it is the bloodstream of what we all do."

Often the first part of IS, usually in the junior year, consists of a seminar or tutorial program that is designed to explore the possible range of research and creative projects in the chosen field and to provide the student with the methodology of research and techniques needed. Seniors then spend two semesters working on their projects that culminate in the writing of a thesis or the production of a substantial creative work. A few recent examples include Synthesis and Evaluation of Cyclohexyl Phosposerine Compounds as Potential Phosolipid Analogs (chemistry); *Le Role D'Une Langue Etrangere Au College En Plein Centre-Ville Aux Estats-Unis* (French); After the Battle: World Trade Organization Labor Policies in the Post-Seattle Era (international relations); Child Abduction in America: A Reflection of Contemporary Society (sociology).

The entire college experience for both faculty and students culminates in this endeavor. Faculty and students work closely together. Each student is assigned a faculty adviser who serves as a mentor, guide, and critic. Learning is thought of as "being collaborative, rather than competitive," allowing neither the faculty member nor the student to have all the answers. Since students are involved in their own education, there is discussion of values and a sense of collegiality. As one faculty member stated, "A relationship builds from an academic situation with a student; then you can move to life questions."

Students and faculty at Wooster told us repeatedly that the IS experience gives them an opportunity beyond the traditional classroom to engage in intellectual discussions with each other, and for students to discover "their identity and what they will do with their life—IS allows questions of values to still be on the table."

At Bethune-Cookman College students are also actively engaged in research projects with faculty. The campus prides itself on the quality of such experiences for students. A recent example is scientific research conducted collaboratively by faculty and students that has resulted in the discovery of an enzyme in the human body that may lead to better treatments for diseases such as Parkinson's,

Alzheimer's, and atherosclerosis. The findings of the research were coauthored and published in a prestigious academic journal.

Summary

The curriculum is the bedrock of a college. It represents what a college values and wants students to learn and experience. The curriculum is shaped by what and how faculty members teach. The colleges in our study focus on the liberal arts to prepare students for careers and to lead meaningful lives. Given the relatively strong church-related missions of some of the colleges in the study, the curriculum is an important vehicle for these campuses to articulate their church's worldview and integrate faith and learning. The following points help to summarize the findings on curriculum:

- Colleges take seriously their mission statements in planning their curriculum. Considerable debate exists at these colleges about what and how to teach.

- Given an emphasis on holistic student development, colleges recognize the importance of creating safe and open classroom environments to foster student learning and development.

- Colleges vary in how purposeful they are in integrating faith and learning inside and outside of the classroom.

- Many colleges use variations of the pedagogy of engagement—service-learning, community-based service and research, January and May terms, study abroad, and student research opportunities—to accomplish their curricular goals for student learning and development.

Questions for Campus Conversations

- *How do you define student learning and development at your institution? What dimensions of student learning and development are emphasized in your campus's academic programs?*

- *How does your institution's mission help to shape your curriculum?*

- *What pedagogies do your institutional leaders support that reinforce the campus's mission and identity?*

- *What resources does your institution offer faculty to design courses and syllabi?*

- *How does your institution support faculty collaboration across disciplines? Are interdisciplinary and multidisciplinary courses part of your core curriculum?*

- *How do your institution's faith tradition, values, and/or worldview(s) influence curricular programming? How does your institution present multiple worldviews and religious traditions to students?*

- *How are faith and learning integrated at your institution? How is this integration enacted?*

- *How do faculty at your institution promote values, character formation, and social and moral responsibility in their teaching?*

5 Cocurriculum

"All accepting and working together to serve and invest our lives in students."

—Faculty member, Union University

"Faculty care about the whole student."

—Faculty member, Whitworth College

Introduction

When we talk about the cocurriculum we are doing so in ways that suggest some connection to the curriculum and that faculty play an important role. The impact of the cocurricular environment on the holistic development of students should not be underestimated. The cocurriculum influences aspects of student life ranging from career choice, to earnings, to educational attainment (Pascarella & Terenzini, 1991). Astin's (1984) theory of involvement focuses on students' connections to different aspects of the college experience and how these experiences shape students and their successes in college. Students who are fully involved in the cocurriculum are likely to persist in college and be academically successful (Kuh, Kinzie, Schuh, Whitt, & Associates, 2005). We also believe that students who are fully involved in the cocurriculum will have richer learning and developmental experiences.

Cocurricular involvement is not just about engaging in multiple activities; instead, it is about becoming involved in activities and organizations that help connect in-class and out-of-class experiences. Student development stands at the intersection of curricular and cocurricular spaces. The cocurricular environment is where students get more fully immersed in particular interests and where they can connect and make meaning out of classroom experiences. The cocurriculum encompasses activities that augment the cognitive and theoretical aspects of the classroom. Student involvement in the cocurriculum can help support the more formal learning embedded in curricular experiences (MacKinnon-Slaney, 1993). These cocurricular experiences take place in locations like the library, computer labs, residence halls, chapels, recreation centers, dining halls, and off campus.

Student affairs practitioners play an important, yet often overlooked, educational role in students' lives, and this role is particularly evident in cocurricular environments. Student affairs practitioners are invaluable to creating campus environments that foster holistic development. The student affairs profession is dedicated to the "development of the whole person" (Nuss, 1996, p. 23), and such development calls for recognizing curricular and cocurricular environments and connections between the two. What we found from our work in this project is that faculty and student affairs professionals play equally important roles in supporting students' holistic development in the cocurricular environment. An administrator at Bethune-Cookman College put it this way: "We need to provide a blend of challenge and support" that involves faculty and staff. As we discussed in Chapter 3, the campuses in this study are marked by a culture of challenge and support, much of which is manifest in cocurricular environments.

We differentiate between two aspects of the cocurriculum: *places* to be involved beyond the classroom, and *activities* to be involved in beyond the classroom. The first relates to environment and where students' lives beyond the classroom take place (e.g., residence halls, faculty offices), and the second is the types of activities that comprise the cocurricular experience (e.g., student government, intramural activities, group projects, volunteer service). The very definition of *co*curriculum suggests simultaneity with the curricular experience; some aspects are closely tied to course work (e.g., study groups) whereas other experiences have an educational component but may only be loosely tied to the curriculum in a formal way (e.g., guest speakers).

The cocurriculum is one of the best ways for students to invest in the campus community. It also is a place where students feel like the campus invests in them. In particular, the cocurriculum is important for developing relationships between faculty and students. It is necessary for students to gain a balance between their interior and exterior lives (Astin, 2004). The *interior* is where students make meaning of issues related to identity, morality, spirituality, values, and the like (issues that are often thought of as personal and private). In contrast, the *exterior* involves the objective, observable behaviors such as those related to classroom learning and student programs (issues that are viewed as more public). Astin argues, and we concur, that there needs to be a greater integration between the interior and exterior, and it is often in the cocurriculum where campuses strike that balance. When such integration and balance take place, students can more forthrightly deal with what might be viewed as personal (e.g., faith development) in public domains like the classroom. Students can then more directly combine cocurricular and curricular experiences. This allows for a fuller collegiate experience, with the cocurriculum providing a richer learning environment and the curriculum including more of the concerns that are typically addressed outside the classroom.

In their cocurricular interactions with students, faculty play an important role in helping students bridge the public and the private (i.e., the interior and exterior) aspects of life. A recurring theme from our research is the importance of out-of-class environments for helping students make meaning of their interior lives, making use of the exterior programs in place. Higher education is one of the "central institutions for young adults in today's world" (Parks, 2000, p. 158), and college campuses are unique places to help students grapple with their purpose in life and the role of a college education in helping them realize their purpose. Faculty and student relationships are the "backbone" of the college experience (Parks, 2000, p. 166), and many of these interactions take place in cocurricular contexts.

Campuses that take seriously the centrality of students' holistic development recognize the importance of the expansive cocurricular environment and the campus community as a whole. Indeed, one does not need to venture far into research and conversation about topics related to student development and student learning to find mention of the integral role of student experiences that take place in the cocurriculum (Kuh et al., 2005; Pascarella & Terenzini, 2005). What we found is that life beyond the classroom is central to student development and success. Faculty at Union University talk about the synergy of the environments: "We have a dynamic learning community, all working together rather than in isolated units. Students want coherent education," and at places like Union they get it.

It is often the cocurricular experiences that relate to learning (e.g., study sessions) but that are beyond the classroom (e.g., in a professor's office) that are most significant for helping students address the bigger questions in life. The findings from our research suggest that the cocurricular experience is manifest in the following environments (i.e., places) and ways (i.e., activities):

- Mutual reinforcement of learning (i.e., living and learning together)
- Campus rituals
- Residence life
- Student leadership
- Relationships with coaches, professional staff, and campus ministry
- Faculty interactions
- Immersion experiences

Mutual Reinforcement of Learning

A central tenet of campus life at the colleges in the study relates to living and learning—what we identify as mutual reinforcement of learning. In the words of a faculty member at The College of Wooster: "We are a laboratory for humanity. We cannot separate students' academic experiences from out of class experiences." Students do not develop holistically without the investment of campus community members, including faculty, and without investment in curricular and cocurricular environments. A holistic approach to student development calls for multiple opportunities for students to be challenged (internally and externally) inside and outside of the classroom (Colby, Ehrlich, Beaumont, & Stephens, 2003).

Mutual reinforcement of learning takes place when living and learning experiences are reinforced throughout the campus environment. Recognizing the importance of the mutual reinforcement of learning, many campuses have developed programs like Freshman Interest Groups and other types of living and learning communities that capitalize on learning opportunities in living arrangements and that take advantage of the community created by living arrangements to enhance learning.

The mutual reinforcement of learning also takes place by creating cocurricular opportunities that help students apply classroom knowledge. A prime example of what we mean by the mutual reinforcement of learning emanates from the Hope College senior seminar (see the profile in Chapter 4). The senior seminar is a capstone core curriculum requirement that asks students to articulate a worldview and how that worldview operates in the context of society and a student's place in society. The classroom aspect of the seminar uses primary texts, short lectures, and plenty of small group discussion. In addition, faculty who teach these courses are invited to monthly dinner meetings where topics relevant to the enrichment of the courses are discussed. The seminar also incorporates local and campus talks as a way to "practice" one's worldview. For example, the subject presented by a guest speaker on campus may be discussed in the classroom, incorporated into the worldview paper, and serve as a springboard for dinner discussion. Further, these conversations are likely to continue into the daily chapel experience and residence halls as well. Members of the capstone class have their learning reinforced through curricular and cocurricular experiences.

We found that out-of-class environments play a very important role in reinforcing what students learn in the classroom. These non-classroom environments are what Kuh et al. (2005) refer to as socially catalytic spaces—places that are socially oriented but key to the learning process; places where learning and development are integrated. What is unique and important about these cocurricular learning spaces is the mutual reinforcement of learning and that the experiences can be facilitated by fellow students, faculty, and/or administrators. Campus events are planned and capitalized on as learning experiences leading to synergy between curricular and cocurricular experiences and ultimately a fuller developmental experience for students. For example, Whitworth College conducted a seminar on Iraq as a "just war." Faculty staged a debate to discuss the war, and students were able to witness the interaction between two prominent faculty with very different points of view about the war as well as participate in the debate. The seminar grew out of, and later returned to, class discussions.

What is it that campuses and faculty, in particular, can do to create such experiences?

- Invite outside speakers cognizant of class topics
- Incorporate current event issues into classroom discussions
- Ask questions to facilitate discussion from classroom, to residence hall, to faculty offices

Campus Rituals

The colleges in our study take seriously and have great participation in campus rituals. Some campuses have deemed campus-wide rituals, like convocation, as outdated traditions. What we found, however, is that events like convocation have been reenvisioned to initiate and set the tone for the academic year. Further, such events help socialize and acculturate students and faculty to the learning environment of the campus. On most of the campuses in the study there was some type of event, such as a convocation or campus picnic, to welcome new and returning students, faculty, and staff. These rituals are also often a place where the campus mission and goals are articulated. Such rituals are not just "nice" things to do—they are important to reinforce the idea of a community of learners where new members are welcomed in a ritualized way. For example, if a campus is focused on integration of thought and action or on faith and learning (themes that were prevalent on the campuses we visited), the fall convocation lecture given by the president might focus on such issues. Subsequently, capstone courses would follow-up on the same, and faculty development initiatives would cover these as well.

Another important aspect of rituals and ceremonics are their importance in celebrating academic achievement. Well-attended commencement ceremonies are obvious celebrations of success. Faculty participation is not viewed as optional at the campuses we studied. Just as it is important for faculty to take part in welcoming students into a learning community, it is also important for them to honor students as they graduate. The vice president for academic affairs at Whitworth College shared with us that commencement is the biggest day of the year on campus and that "students can't wait for the faculty to meet their parents." In addition, faculty at Whitworth line the sidewalk and applaud the students as they enter the graduation ceremonies. Such involvement makes clear the conscious and deliberate role faculty play in student life.

In addition to the more formalized events, we also learned about rituals that are unique to individual campuses. For example, the "Tootsie Roll Handout" at The College of Wooster celebrates the completion of the independent study (IS) project (see profile in Chapter 4). What started as a fun and trivial exercise has come to mark an important rite of passage for Wooster students. When students complete their senior IS projects, they are given a Tootsie Roll and "parade" with faculty to celebrate. Every member of the campus community knows about the "Tootsie Roll Handout." It symbolizes an important developmental milestone for students and their faculty advisors.

Campus rituals can be used to:

- Create the feeling of community
- Welcome new members to the campus
- Reinforce classroom goals
- Celebrate academic rites of passage and achievements

Residence Life

Since a majority of liberal arts colleges are residential in nature (i.e., most students live on campus and those who do not tend to live near campus), residence life programs play a prominent role in the cocurriculum. The very term *residence hall*, which has replaced the previously used term *dormitory*, captures the essence of its impact on holistic student development: Residence halls are places to live and learn. We found that residence halls are important sites where resident assistants (undergraduate students) and hall directors (professional staff) play key roles in student learning and development. Residence halls are where living and learning come together—a key tenet of holistic student development. Most campuses, in our study and elsewhere, go to great lengths to capitalize on the learning and development opportunities that can and are created in residence halls, given their educative value (Kuh, 1993; Pascarella & Terenzini, 1991). To do otherwise is artificial, and as the vice president of student affairs at Hope College told us, "You cannot just compartmentalize. Residential life challenges us to integrate."

How is the cocurriculum manifest in residence halls as part of holistic student development? In our research we found that residence halls have an impact in four major ways:

- Residence halls are places of cocurricular learning
- Issues in residence halls come into the classrooms and vice versa
- Residence life personnel and their role in cultivating holistic student development
- Organized living and learning communities

Residence Halls Are Places of Cocurricular Learning

It is not surprising that residence halls are places where students form study groups and special interest meetings (e.g., Bible studies) as a way to augment in-class learning. In line with the concept of a learning community, even an activity that is seemingly not tied to the curriculum becomes a learning experience for students. For example, at Whitworth College, Bible studies can be found on a nightly basis in residence halls on campus. These Bible studies are unique because they are initiated and run by students. Moreover, they create opportunities for students to grapple with connections between faith and learning. Students told us that it is often in Bible studies where questions related to classroom topics are discussed to figure out how a particular biblical concept might connect to a disciplinary one. On most of the campuses that we visited, students and faculty participate in Bible studies together, making these groups an important connection point for students and faculty. At Union University, the same type of interaction takes place in a campus book club, where faculty and students read the same book and then discuss it in out-of-class settings that include residence halls. This gives students greater access to outside learning opportunities, which ultimately foster student development and success (Pascarella & Terenzini, 1991, 2005).

Issues in Residence Halls Come Into the Classrooms and Vice Versa

Residence halls are not only places of learning; they also generate topics of learning. For example, at some of the campuses we visited, we learned that residence halls were not comfortable places for students who considered themselves "different." In one instance, a student in a residence hall found the environment to be a challenge because she did not practice Christianity in the same way as some of her peers; at one point she found students praying in front of her door. This situation came to the attention of a faculty member and made its way into a religious studies class where the professor talked about what it means to be a Christian in name and practice. Residence halls are prime locations for teachable moments, and issues that surfaced in the halls were often discussed in the classroom. In this way residence halls create synergy. The provost at Creighton University had this to say: "What happens in class is then replayed a thousand times in the dorms and the impact of what happens in student residence life hits every classroom the next day."

Residence Life Personnel and Their Role in Cultivating Holistic Student Development

Another important aspect of residence life and holistic student development is the role of residence life personnel, namely, resident assistants (RAs) and hall directors. Faculty and students repeatedly mentioned these individuals as essential to student life and development. Most of the campuses we visited talked of the need to hire residence life personnel who are uniquely qualified to help students integrate living and learning. Training is an important part of taking advantage of the educative moments that occur in the residence hall, and the campuses in the study were careful to prepare their residence life personnel for the types of issues they may encounter.

We also found that the term *resident assistant* can be broadly defined. For example, at Creighton University, Jesuits live in the residence halls and help students deal with interpersonal conflicts that can arise in living communities. But they are also available to discuss classroom topics with students and to help students make meaning of some of the larger life transitions that occur during the college experience. Campuses with faculty and other staff in residence halls send a strong message of the connections that are desired between living and learning. We heard repeatedly of the importance of a professional presence in residence halls.

- *Hire for fit.* If residence life personnel are to assist students in making connections between living and learning, purposeful hiring can help them be prepared to do so.

- *Staff development can prepare residence life personnel to assist in meeting campus goals* (e.g., integration of faith and learning). If something controversial is being discussed in the classroom, it is also likely to show up in the residence hall. Prepared staff are better able to take advantage of such teachable moments.

- *Synergy between residence life staff and faculty helps to cultivate living and learning communities.*

Organized Living and Learning Communities

Increasingly popular on college campuses are living environments that are organized around some nucleus of interest. For example, at The College of Wooster, students can arrange to live together around a commitment to a mutual service project. At Hope College and Whitworth College, students can propose to live together around any unified interest (e.g., Spanish houses). Creighton University provides a living and learning environment where students participate in service projects for the campus and for the city of Omaha as well as seminar-type discussions. The University of Dayton offers unique living arrangements by year in school in an effort to create living environments that encourage learning relative to stages of student development.

Often these arranged living situations are co-inhabited by residence life staff and faculty. Such arrangements are commonplace on college campuses—public and private, large and small—across the country and attest to the importance of viewing the campus environment holistically, where valuable learning takes place in living environments and where living environments generate learning opportunities. At the University of Dayton, many of the Marianist brothers and priests live in small religious communities that are interspersed among the houses and apartments of upper-class students. This allows students to visit with faculty in their homes if they find they need to talk to someone about their classes or their future. The ethos of living and learning at Dayton is highlighted in the following profile.

Profile

University of Dayton

The introduction to the brochure "Our Community: Written for Students, by Students" states, "The community that exists on our campus is very intentional; it is an essential component of the Marianist culture on campus." A Marianist university is "founded around the principle of service through education." The campus ethos reflects the motto "learn, lead, and serve." It is a way of living and does not need to be particularly religious in expressing how one can live out this theme. It does stress engagement in the larger world, solving problems, and caring for others. Students, faculty, and staff often used the following words to describe the university: community, friendly, family, caring, hospitality, inclusiveness, openness to all faiths and ethnic backgrounds, egalitarianism, practical in orientation and outlook, social, building community.

About 95% of the students live on campus all four years. The housing arrangements at Dayton recognize that different stages of student development can call for different types of housing and that certain housing configurations create different types of community. Freshmen live in traditional-type residence halls (double rooms on a corridor with communal bath facilities) situated in the core of the campus area. Sophomores participate in a housing lottery for assignments to a four-person suite, a six-person apartment high-rise, a four-person garden apartment, or a return to a traditional residence hall. Juniors typically live in apartment facilities in the south residential neighborhood or seek out landlord-owned houses. Seniors get first pick of the university-owned houses in three distinct neighborhoods—Ghetto, North, and Holy Angels (named after the local Catholic parish). Since most of these homes have porches, a "porch culture" has been established, signifying "welcomeness" to all students.

Dayton takes the concept of living and learning seriously. It fosters a living and learning environment that reflects the Marianist worldview and has recently constructed two new buildings with space that reinforces this concept. In Marianist Hall, the first floor contains the bookstore and space for social interactions. The second floor is 10,000 square feet of flexible learning space, fully equipped with the latest technology. Students who live on the same floors can attend classes right in the building to increase interaction among the students. "It is so Marianist," one faculty member stated. The other recently opened space is the Art Street Building, located in the midst of the "Ghetto" housing units—blocks of old homes purchased by the university for senior student housing. The building displays the artwork of students, faculty, and artists, and students who are not art majors take art classes there. It took four years of meetings among students, student affairs, academic affairs, and ministry to design the space to reflect the mission of the university (i.e., a living and learning environment that meets the total needs of the students). For example, there is a student-run coffee shop where students can gather, mingle, and learn together. Alumni, students, staff, and faculty all talk about the porch culture as Dayton's signature. Community is designed and nurtured. Dayton is intentional about it.

Student Leadership

Generally speaking, students at the campuses we studied are an empowered and involved group. Opportunities to assume leadership roles help develop an ethos of self-responsibility among students. For example, at Whitworth College, students are able to propose ideas they have for programs ranging from themed housing to off-campus service projects. Students put together proposals based on ideas they believe would augment and reinforce student learning and development. The proposals are then considered (typically by a committee of student affairs practitioners and faculty), and decisions to approve proposals are based, in part, on their contribution to holistic student development.

As part of our research site visits, we participated, when possible, in chapel programs. Based on what we observed, it was evident that these programs are also largely driven by student interests, and follow-up interviews confirmed that students initiate and lead chapel programs. At Hope, the chapel leader on the day of our visit was a student relaying international perspectives, how a global view of society was necessary in order to succeed in the world, and how her experience at Hope had prepared her to meet the challenges of living in a global society. The student's chapel presentation epitomized for us the integration of curricular and cocurricular contexts.

The chapel program at Hope College merits additional comment. It is largely student-focused and provides numerous opportunities for student participation in leadership. Chapel was mentioned as an important element of the cocurriculum by everyone we spoke with at the college. That roughly half of the student body voluntarily attends the chapel program is remarkable, and we attribute this participation to the high level of student involvement in creating the chapel experience. The chapel is integral to helping form relationships among students and develops a sense of community on campus. When talking about the chapel, students mentioned the importance of the chapel for listening to music and seeing friends, whereas some faculty and administrators desired chapel to be more focused on depth and reflection. Regardless, chapel services are a source of connection among faculty, staff, and students. In chapel, relationships are important and central—when at chapel, who a person is and what their position is dissipates. Student plans are instrumental to create the chapel experience, and the chapel is striving to be a source of community for all members of Hope, not just students.

A downside to students taking on leadership roles in the cocurriculum is over-involvement—a topic not often discussed. Students at the campuses we visited are an involved group, but sometimes that can work against the intellectual life of the campus. As one faculty member commented, "Students are over-committed . . . it's the culture to be service oriented," and for some students this means service to the campus through student group participation and leadership as well as active involvement in community service projects beyond the campus. A characteristic of millennial students, as described by Howe and Strauss (2003), is active involvement in groups and clubs. Millennials are joiners. Faculty at Union University, the University of Dayton, and Villanova University, in particular, lamented the fact that too much joining can compromise the quality of student classroom work, with some students putting their studies second to participation in campus activities, local churches, and service projects.

Relationships With Coaches, Professional Staff, and Campus Ministry

The purpose of this book is to highlight faculty involvement in student development, but our study also revealed that coaches, professional staff, and campus ministry play important roles in students' lives. Typically, the way campuses are organized means that the domain of the staff in student affairs is cocurriculum and the domain of the faculty is curriculum. However, we found considerable blurring of these boundaries in the colleges we visited. We discovered that lessons learned on the athletic playing field or in retreats often reinforce holistic student development.

Relationships with coaches, professional staff, and campus ministry in the cocurriculum environment help foster student development in three ways:

- Character formation
- Opportunity for performance
- Support and challenge

Character Formation

The cocurriculum environment is where issues associated with character formation and developing a sense of purpose beyond that of promoting individual successes are often directly manifested. Being part of a team to learn cooperation and group work and creating a sense of purpose is what many athletes experience in college. In this study students involved in athletics mentioned synergy between the playing field and classroom. Coaches, many of whom have a teaching role as well, spoke of the need to make certain that playing in competitive sports supports goals, such as fair play, persistence, and performance under pressure. Coaches work with students to be good sports and to recognize that winning isn't always possible. The same is true in the classroom. Good sportsmanship is a form of development and, in some instances, is more important than winning (Davis, 1987).

A coach at The College of Wooster talked with us about how it is essential for team members to work well together. This can result in winning, but the real value she wants to impart to her students is that of working together. A coach and professor of physical education at the University of Dayton provided another example of character formation: Emphasizing and role modeling such behaviors as dressing for the occasion, respecting the opposing team, and teamwork are a large part of the student experience.

Opportunity for Performance

Cocurricular and extracurricular activities create opportunities for students to be involved in life beyond the classroom, and many of these opportunities include some aspect of performance. Students perform in many places—speaking in chapel, singing in the choir, and playing athletics. When students perform in these public forums, they are often learning and practicing leadership skills. Students gain valuable experience in displaying their talents with public audiences. The chair of the music department explained that the myriad musical programs offered at Pacific Lutheran University allow students to become involved in activities that augment their classroom experience by imparting important lessons. The professional caliber of these programs helps students learn the importance of professional preparation and performance, see the development of a project from beginning to end, and witness the creative process. Musical events are often presented internationally (e.g., the choir at Hope College annually travels to places around the world, allowing students to learn about life in another culture). The time spent organizing, practicing, and performing in professional venues means significant interaction beyond the classroom with the staff and faculty who lead these programs. Faculty and staff work closely with students, and it is these faculty and staff who students mention when they talk about their college experience.

As discussed in the section on student leadership, chapel programs are an important part of campus life at some of the institutions we studied. These programs are largely initiated and run by students and provide opportunities for them to share their skills and talents with the campus community. Students are instrumental in crafting aspects of the experience that include inviting outside speakers, setting up technology, and performing in chapel services. Again, much of this is done in relation with campus ministry and other staff, leading to the development of meaningful relationships.

Support and Challenge

On college campuses it is often the faculty who challenge students and student affairs professionals who provide support. But what we found at the campuses we studied is a blurring of these traditional boundaries. Creating a climate of challenge and support is a collective responsibility. For example, at The College of Wooster, we interviewed a group of female students on the swim team who described their swimming coach as providing them with support and challenge. He encouraged them in their athletic prowess and challenged them in their academic endeavors by sharing his own personal journey. We found significant synergy between students' involvement in cocurricular programs and their lives in the classroom. Student interactions with coaches, professional staff, and ministry play an important role in challenging students to be their best in the classroom and in other settings.

Faculty Interactions

Faculty involvement is a key component of college student development (Pascarella & Terenzini, 1991, 2005). The interactions between faculty and students in the cocurricular environment develop trust and rapport. Faculty come to see students as colleagues, but this only takes place over time and through mutual investment in the relationship. Given the collaborative culture we encountered on the campuses we studied, there is much contact between faculty and students. Students frequent faculty offices and often work together with faculty on campus initiatives and programs in both academic matters such as research and in student leadership programs. The relationships that develop between faculty and students play an important role in students' holistic development. When faculty and students become invested in one another, it creates a more conducive environment for faculty to challenge students and to become more involved in student development. It is also easier to encourage students when faculty have developed rapport with them. To get to this point calls for frequent and in-depth interaction between faculty and students. Faculty also serve as mentors and role models to students (Parks, 2000). Parks refers to college campuses as mentoring communities and as places where young adults—in this case, college students—can search for meaning in life.

Where and how do faculty and student interactions take place? The classroom is one important place, but from the perspective of students, far more important are the informal interactions faculty have with students in places like dining areas, residence halls, office hours, and faculty homes. In our research, we found the latter two to be mentioned more frequently with regard to faculty involvement in fostering holistic student development.

Office Hours

When we asked students and faculty where their most meaningful interactions take place—interactions that we would classify as holistic—faculty office hours were by far the most prevalent response. Office hours provide students with the opportunity to receive extra help on class problems, and in terms of student development, it is in office hours where students feel more free to ask faculty about the big questions in life and where they often have "a-ha" moments about topics covered in the formal classroom setting. Our interviews revealed that faculty sometimes augment classroom discussions with more personal information. For example, in class, faculty often do not want to reveal too many personal viewpoints on a particular topic for fear that they will stymie student critical thinking. Students sometimes want to get "right" answers, and faculty giving personal opinions on particular issues can prevent students from arriving at their own conclusions on a particular issue. In office hours, however, faculty told us that they felt more open to telling students more about their particular perspective on a given topic. One example that stands out is a Whitworth College faculty member presenting in class about the "geography of place." In one class session, several students were grappling with national policies related to the environment. Wanting students to explore all sides of the topic, the faculty member did not share his particular viewpoints at the outset, but in follow-up office hours he felt more open about sharing his personal views. In this way he was able to engage students more fully in their own critical thinking without having students feel pressure to articulate their positions in relation to the professor's. Office hour conversations often lead to other topics of interest and concern and are where "real thinking" and development can take place.

Faculty also reserve office hour time (as opposed to class time) to talk about the intersection of faith and learning. We were surprised by students' eagerness to talk about controversial topics in class (e.g., gay marriage, presidential elections, race relations). While faculty are, for the most part, happy to engage such topics as long as they are related to the class topic, they are often unsure of how to keep the conversation going. It was not uncommon on such class days to have office hours significantly augment class discussions to help students deal with the material in personal, intellectual, and, many times, church-related contexts. As a result, office hour interactions help faculty and students develop holistic relationships. The rapport developed during office hours creates greater involvement in the classroom and allows students to feel a more personal connection to faculty. As a student from Pacific Lutheran University stated, "Faculty know the details of your life . . . they are not just professors. They have a willingness to take an interest in my life and go out of the way to help me." For this student, such relationships with faculty developed largely in office hour discussions.

Recognizing the importance of office hours, the Villanova Institute for Teaching and Learning (VITAL) established a brown-bag lunch discussion about how to make the best use of office hours. A description of this brown-bag session is as follows:

> Faculty office hours have many purposes, all of which are aimed at helping our students succeed in our courses. So why is it such a struggle to get students to take advantage of office hours? Even when students do appear, there can still be challenges: Figuring out how best to help them as individuals, dealing with personal issues that may be beyond our responsibilities or expertise, or even coping with the inevitable interruptions from phone calls, colleagues, and other students. How do we make office hours an effective use of everyone's time?

Valuable student development takes place during office hours. Villanova's faculty development brown bag is an ideal way to help faculty make the best use of their time. At the colleges in this study, faculty are expected to be available for office hours. Some lessons we learned from the interviews on the topic of office hours include:

- Stay true to office hour postings.
- Have students sign up for office hours so there is plenty of time to address their concerns.
- Give examples of the types of concerns students bring to office hour discussions (e.g., career ideas, class help) and provide insight on how to address common concerns.
- Some office interactions can bring up personal issues (e.g., mental or physical health concerns) that are beyond faculty expertise. Faculty familiarity of their boundaries in terms of

helping students and knowledge of the resources to direct students to more personalized and professional help is useful.

- Faculty should be aware of proper etiquette and the appropriateness of office hour topics, given what can be viewed as an intimate setting between faculty and students. Some campuses have found it helpful to include such issues in faculty orientation sessions and other types of faculty development (e.g., the Villanova brown-bag discussion).

Faculty Homes

Similar to office hours, our study revealed that faculty homes are an important site of cocurricular learning. Many faculty live close to campus with the specific intent of hosting students at their homes as part of the holistic learning experience. For example, faculty spoke of regularly scheduled dinners at their homes for students in particular classes. But these interactions are not limited to dinner nor are they class specific. For example, at Hope College, a faculty member has regular breakfast meetings with students, and at the University of Dayton some of the Marianist priests invite students to their homes for discussion and conversation. Such interactions are very important to the student experience and were referred to repeatedly by many students. In faculty homes, students get a better sense of who the faculty member is as a person, which in turn helps students to think of themselves more fully. Given the goal of holistic student development to meld the different aspects of student life, faculty homes provide an inside glimpse at how faculty integrate the different aspects of their lives. As one faculty member put it, "Students like to see the other side of faculty, such as their spouse and children."

In our interviews, we learned that academic leaders encourage faculty to live close to campus in an effort to create greater fluidity between campus and community. This allows students to visit faculty homes and also contributes to a close-knit community in general. On some campuses, however, leaders noted the difficulties of faculty living close to campus, given the cost and character of campus neighborhood environments, especially in more urban areas. For example, at Pacific Lutheran University, faculty are migrating away from campus neighborhoods, which contributed to investors buying homes for rental properties, further lessening the appeal for faculty to live in these neighborhoods. Pacific Lutheran has recently reinvested in the neighborhood surrounding the campus in the hope that faculty will move back closer to the university to help connect the campus and the community. In the interim, Pacific Lutheran provides transportation for students via buses to faculty homes for faculty dinners. This attests to the importance they give to faculty and student interaction in a home environment, which can often be more genuine than in other settings.

Inviting students to a faculty member's home is not just about faculty being "nice." Perhaps more importantly, and often overlooked, is the vital role that personal interactions between faculty and students play in the developmental process—an important part of the cocurricular experience. Ultimately, faculty and student interactions are about learning and development. What is clear from our research is that this development takes place in multiple settings. Not all faculty can, or desire, to invite students to their home, and faculty investment in holistic student development does not require such interactions. Some faculty feel strongly about keeping boundary lines. What we did find, however, is the interactions that take place in faculty homes are memorable developmental milestones for students. The private and public boundaries that can exist between faculty and students can dissipate in off-campus faculty home environments.

Faculty and student interactions in home settings are important learning experiences. Campuses can be deliberate and supportive of faculty inviting students to their homes in the following ways:

- Encourage faculty to think about the type of interaction they want to have with students and to consider housing options that will help support this.
- Offer incentives for faculty to live close to campus.
- Provide funds to help faculty host students at their homes.
- Supply transportation needed to prompt at least periodic interactions between students and faculty in a home setting.
- Provide campus venues for faculty to interact with students in homey environments (e.g., student lounges, dining hall areas that are set apart) to create places that foster the informal interactions students seek with faculty.

Immersion Experiences

Our research revealed numerous examples of faculty, students, and sometimes staff collectively participating in immersion experiences. At Creighton University, retreats were a common source of immersion, with departments gathering for days or weekends to focus on new initiatives and build community between and among faculty and students. A source of immersion at the University of Dayton is the "urban plunge," where groups of students and faculty participate in weekend service experiences in urban environments. At Whitworth College, an Amtrak trip that is part of the course "Prejudice Across America" allows students to participate with a faculty member in a cultural train excursion. Students who participate in this unique course learn concepts and facts, but the character of the course is immersion, and for students, this is what stands out about the class.

Immersion experiences sometimes emanate from the curriculum (e.g., study abroad programs), but they have very important and significant cocurricular aspects. For the student and faculty member on a study abroad experience in Costa Rica, a large part of the day is spent in class focused on study topics, but important interactions and mentoring take place in the evenings, in between study sites, and while traveling. A Pacific Lutheran University student who participated in a study abroad program to Belize mentioned that it was during that experience when she realized the faculty member leading the trip was a "whole person with a family, friends, and concerns."

Undergraduate research experiences also provide students with opportunities to immerse themselves in projects and in close interactions with faculty. Without exception, the campuses in our study are actively working to further develop student and faculty cooperation in research projects. These experiences are often tied to the curriculum and have come to be expected as part of the undergraduate experience. For example, The College of Wooster requires all students to complete an undergraduate research project where they work closely with faculty members on independent study projects. The immersion aspect of these research projects is the amount of time students put into their research and the amount of time they work with faculty as a result of doing so. These projects can sometimes take place over an extended period of time. In particular, faculty at Whitworth College and Hope College talked of hiring students for summer research projects, which provides an opportunity for students to learn more about the nuances of research as well as a specific project. In addition, such experiences typically create very close working relationships between faculty and students. For the faculty involved in such experiences, they talked of the close connections they develop with the students with whom they do research, often continuing to work with them in graduate school and/or working with some students over an extended period of time. For the students involved in intensive research experiences, they simultaneously learn the intricacies of research while getting the opportunity to work more closely with a particular faculty member. They witness firsthand how faculty combine career with vocation and balance their professional and personal lives. Such interactions put faculty and students into long-term relationships that often continue long after graduation.

We repeatedly heard about the learning, development, and relationship building that occurs in the spaces between formal learning activities. It is often the conversations that take place to and from a more formal learning (e.g., study abroad) or cocurricular experience (e.g., a service project) where authentic learning moments occur. These spaces allow students to make connections between course content and the real world, and between the public and the private. As one faculty member stated, "I do my best teaching in the van." These interactions tend to be more authentic and are meaningful to students and faculty alike. Informal interactions that take place between faculty and students in cocurricular environments are crucial to holistic student development.

Summary

The cocurricular environment is about places to interact—resident halls, faculty offices—and people to interact with—namely, faculty, professional staff, residence hall staff, coaches, and campus ministers. As we close this chapter, we want to highlight the importance of relationships in creating meaningful cocurricular interactions. People make the difference in helping students connect the cocurricular context with other aspects of the undergraduate experience. In particular, we found the following experiences and places instrumental to augment student development:

- Office hours (formal and informal).
- Faculty homes and other off-campus locations.
- Study abroad programs accompanied by faculty where the curriculum and cocurriculum intersect.

- Immersion experiences (e.g., faculty accompanying students on service trips for spring break).
- Summer research experiences where students help faculty with their research.
- Field and lab settings.
- Undergraduate research experiences that call for one-on-one interactions between faculty and students.

Questions for Campus Conversations

- *How are curricular and cocurricular environments connected at your institution?*
- *How do you encourage and prepare faculty at your institution to work with students in the cocurricular context?*
- *What opportunities are available at your institution to encourage living and learning together?*
- *What campus rituals are considered to be essential in portraying the character and identity of your institution, developing a sense of tradition, and bringing the community together to celebrate? What role do they play in fostering student development?*
- *Do residence hall staff and faculty at your institution interact to think purposefully about the interface of living and learning and development?*
- *What role do student-initiated programs and student leadership programs play in student development at your institution?*

- *How would you describe the character and nature of faculty and student interactions at your institution? What supports are in place to foster these relationships? What challenges inhibit the relationships?*

- *What opportunities do students at your institution have to immerse themselves in curricular and cocurricular projects? Are you taking advantage of formal academic year programs to offer immersion experiences? How are faculty members participating in these immersion experiences? How can you encourage more faculty, staff, and students to become involved?*

6 Community

"Learning in community, for community, and as a community [is emphasized here]."

—Dean, University of Dayton

"You can just feel the community here . . . it's palpable."

—Faculty member, Whitworth College

Introduction

The subject of community is no stranger to higher education. McDonald (2002) defines community as the policies and practices that mark the distinctive mission of a collegiate institution and that accent the shared values and commitments held in common by institutional constituents. Palmer (1987) identifies community as an inward capacity for relatedness to people and all parts of the world. Institutions that lack community are described by Astin (1993) as having infrequent socializing among students, little student interaction outside of class, and a high degree of student apathy. Sometimes a community is difficult to establish when students are being pulled in different directions in their academic, extracurricular, social, and personal lives (Boyer, 1990a). In this chapter we refer to community in two general ways. First, the college community can describe the character of the campus and the relationships that develop within a context of camaraderie and collegiality. Second, community can refer to the external relationships colleges and universities have with the communities beyond the campus.

Community as a descriptor of the campus in general attempts to capture the essence of the culture and climate of a campus (e.g., "this campus has a coherent community") as well as the members of a campus (e.g., "we are all members of the campus community"). The notion of community conjures images of collaboration and the sense of a collective effort to create a campus culture that is welcoming and inclusive of all members. Although community is shaped by the culture of the campus and the norms that dictate how and the extent to which people interact (Kuh & Whitt, 1988), it is distinct from the culture of the campus that we discussed in Chapter 3. Whereas culture refers to the overall impact of the underlying mission and focus of the institution, community describes the working relationships and ensuing sense of unity that develops. Community is about what people do to create hospitable places to work and study (Bennett, 2003) and how the campus community interacts with external communities.

In this study, talk of community on campus permeated each of our site visits. The following are phrases we heard from faculty, students, and administrators that capture the essence of the internal campus aspects of community:

- "The campus community is close knit."
- "We are a community of learners here."
- "We are all members of a campus community."
- "The sense of community is so incredible here."
- "The campus is an open community."
- "I love it here, I love the community."
- "We don't want to dilute the sense of community here."
- "We need to develop a sense of community and involve all campus members."
- "We are a highly relational and caring campus community . . . we are 'high touch'."
- "We are known as a community-oriented place."

We highlight the concept of community because the campus community in turn shapes and facilitates faculty involvement in holistic student development. A recurring theme we heard from the people we interviewed was related to the need for students to feel a part of the community in order for them to learn and develop. Development is a relational process among students, faculty, and staff and needs to be cultivated in a climate, culture, and community that is supportive and challenging. A faculty member at Union University said it best: "What we learn is learned in the context of community and in shared relationships with one another. Thus we live and learn in relationship."

The campus environment has an impact on how and what students develop, as well as their interactions with faculty. We learned that campuses are deliberate in creating community and welcoming new members into the community. Students, and the importance of creating communities where student development and learning are foremost on campus, are essential to the institutions we studied. For example, the president of Villanova University was very clear in his communication about creating community to "educate students." He deliberately uses *education* as an encompassing term that goes far beyond what students learn. Community cultivates the teaching and learning process, but, more importantly, it creates a sociocultural environment that fosters holistic student development. Community is not just about being "nice" and "getting along." It is the bedrock to creating an ethos of inquiry and scholarship. Part of what makes a higher education community distinct from other types of communities (e.g., church) is this commitment to academic inquiry (Ferguson & Weston, 2003). But these communities still have a moral character.

> Morality on campus today is . . . formed and shaped in *dialogue*. . . . Respect for the autonomy of students does not entail surrender to a wholly individualistic conception of morality. . . . We are moral beings because we are beings who live in community and

> who shape our ideals in dialogue. (Hoekema, 1994, p. 164)

Dykstra (1999) calls for colleges and universities to act as "communities of conviction" (p. 129) that are not only dedicated to inquiry but also to a set of shared values, religious traditions, and worldviews, and have common rituals to reinforce shared perspectives. Communities of conviction create a climate to assist students in their development. Some of the colleges we studied are easily characterized as communities of conviction, owing largely to their respective church-related legacies. We note, however, that this concept can be extended to include secular notions of shared values as well. For example, Boyer (1990a) calls for six principles to guide campuses in creating communities that foster faculty and student interactions. These principles include a call for a campus community that is educationally purposeful, open, just, disciplined, caring, and celebrative. Such shared values can help a campus in its quest for holistic student development.

Campus community is also about caring—letting students know that they matter to faculty and staff. "Keeping students at the center" is a goal we often heard. Cohesive campus communities are better able to be available for students and to contribute to their development. The "early alert system" at Hamline University is a prime example of how this works. The system involves all offices, including financial aid personnel and residence life, since they see the interconnectedness of a student's problem with their studies. As one staff person said, "If you keep students at the center of the community it is evident how to structure services for students." This caring also is linked to being responsible and accountable. Faculty and staff who care are not indifferent; they extend themselves to help others, often at their own personal and professional expense. Students often mention individuals (e.g., faculty advisor) who go out of their way to make them feel at home, provide comfort in time of family difficulties and sadness, and reassure them when they feel overwhelmed.

Shared Governance

Shinn (2004) argues that liberal arts colleges, such as those in our study, are shaped by a mission-driven governance model. That is, campuses think seriously about their mission as leaders, and faculty make decisions and plan for the future. At these colleges, students stand at the forefront of decision-making. We repeatedly heard of the call for a focus on "what's good for students" as a way to make organizational, programmatic, and curricular decisions. Such intentionality makes these campuses good places to work and to learn. Faculty are involved in decision-making and participate in the focus and direction of the campus.

Faculty play a prominent role in developing and maintaining community. They should be encouraged to become involved in the development and maintenance of the campus, and they should be rewarded for their involvement. For example, the internal character of the institutions in our study relies on faculty playing an active role in shared governance and the smooth functioning of the campus. For campuses to function effectively with external constituencies they need to first be functional internally (Berberet, 2002; Ward, 2003). Our research revealed a very active group of faculty who are committed to the institution and its mission and identity. Faculty work hard to create a sociocultural environment necessary to foster holistic student development. For example, faculty at Hope College talked of department meetings focused on the improvement of teaching and the need to develop good teaching among faculty to contribute to holistic student development.

Collaborative campus climates help create a collective responsibility for teaching and learning instead of deferring to others to create community. That is, faculty see it as their responsibility to create community for students in the same way that student affairs administrators do. We talked to staff who expressed the need to contribute to creating a welcoming environment for students. Generally, those with whom we spoke (faculty, staff, administrators, students) all referred to the community orientation of their campuses as fundamental to their feeling a part of the institution—a prevalent theme of this book. Community and its creation and maintenance are not a trivial matter at these campuses. Given the church-related mission of the universities in the study, community has the added element of regular expressions of their respective faith traditions. These common traditions also help to create an ethos of community.

Creating community—a community where faculty involvement in student development is supported—calls for collective responsibility. Faculty and staff mentioned that being part of a community means stepping outside oneself. As we have already suggested, faculty play a key role in this. We also learned that students play central roles in maintaining the campus community. Students are empowered and often provide input on the direction of the campus. This merits comment on two fronts: The students interviewed were highly involved in the campus community, and this involvement connects them with faculty. Faculty, students, and administrators work side by side as part of shared governance. This is not how we typically think of shared governance, but is characteristic of these campuses nevertheless. For example, students at Creighton University have a voice in budgetary decisions. Student representation is typical on initiatives that affect the campus as a whole. Such involvement contributes to student development and promotes faculty and student interaction, which helps build strong relationships. One concern that was raised about student involvement in decision-making is that it means students can get over-involved and not spend enough time on their studies. There was also concern raised by faculty and students that the student voice is given “lip service,” but student input is not always considered equally to faculty and staff.

Another aspect of the internal community that is important to fostering faculty involvement in holistic student development is the collaborative nature of a campus and the feeling of collective responsibility to foster campus community. We heard repeatedly about putting students at the center of the educational process and doing what needs to be done to address their needs. What this means is that academic affairs and student affairs work collaboratively, for the most part, to approach holistic student development. Putting students and the good of the community at the center can help to overcome individual differences. It is not our intention to glorify interactions between academic affairs and student affairs. In fact, on one campus in particular, people we interviewed talked about the historic rifts between the two offices (although the tension is beginning to dissipate as a more collaborative approach is being tried). What merits consideration is how, even on this campus, engaging in a strategic planning process run by mixed groups of faculty, staff, students, and administrators helped to break down barriers in the interest of the mission and direction of the campus. Campus stakeholders realize a collaborative approach is more helpful than a divided one if the campus is to accomplish its goals. Shared governance is broadly defined at these campuses and includes all voices—faculty, staff, students, and administration.

Both academic and student affairs leaders noted how the two offices can model how to work together collaboratively and with a community orientation. A holistic approach to student development is likely to be more successful if the different functional areas of academic and student affairs are viewed more holistically as well. Leaders often spoke of the desire to be more collaborative; one administrator referred to the connection as "seamless." The bottom line for Pacific Lutheran University was to "stress working together" and "it starts at the top." A faculty member at Whitworth College put it this way: "It's a community effort to educate the students. It requires student affairs and academic affairs to work together in fostering the development of students. It requires a commitment to break out of the silos."

While we have focused thus far on how campus community fosters connectedness and development for students, we also learned that the community promotes a sense of connectedness for faculty. Faculty talked openly about how the strong sense of community kept them on campus. Many faculty came to campus thinking they would remain only for a couple of years, just to get established, but then decided to stay and had long and fruitful careers because of the community orientation of the campus. For example, a faculty member at Hamline University said,

> People come and they stay. When I came here, I thought I was going to be at the university for a few years, but the sense of community was something I hadn't expected—working collectively, the sense of colleagueship that was rewarding and satisfying, and openness and acceptance. Friendliness does not necessarily equal sense of community. It's supportedness.

Faculty at Whitworth College were also forthcoming about the impact the community had on their staying in their positions. And those who do leave lament the loss of community. Departed colleagues often say, "You don't realize what you have there until you leave. It's a unique environment." From a faculty development standpoint, a sense of community for faculty is important to develop and maintain.

At the campuses in our study, the internal service faculty engage in helps to maintain the character and community of the campus. This community helps to foster faculty involvement in student development and learning by creating an environment that impacts students (Finsen, 2002). We found that faculty are hard at work on projects to help enliven and rethink different aspects of campus life. Many institutions had either just recently completed major campus-wide planning initiatives or were in the process of doing so. At Creighton University, for example, departmental retreats inclusive of faculty and students were used to talk about curricular directions of programs. The retreats create shared ownership of the direction of departments.

Defining Community

Many of the initiatives that were underway at the institutions we studied took a deliberate look at what it means to be a member of the campus community. But what is *campus community* exactly? It's a term we hear (and heard) repeatedly, but we are not always clear what it means. Faculty and students spoke about it as an embodiment of the campus. That is, the campus is a community. Intrigued by the overuse of the term *community*, an administrator from Creighton University had this to say:

> I have breakfast every Wednesday morning with students. They love the sense of community. That is an overused word, so I always ask, "What do you mean by that?" They say everybody talks with everybody else. Everybody is friendly. Everybody is supportive. They walk across campus and people smile and wave at them. We are small enough to do that. And the fact that undergraduate freshmen can talk to a third year medical student [that is community]. Which is not just role modeling for them but also instructional and mentoring. We built a new science building that connects the undergraduate science building with the medical school. There is a huge lounge, which is filled everyday with freshmen intermingling with professional students. I think that sense of community is very much here.

Comments such as these were echoed throughout our visits. Community means working together and creating hospitable environments that foster student development. Community also means intentionally creating times, places, and spaces for faculty and students to authentically connect as colleagues, co-learners, mentors/mentees, and teachers/students. This relates to the cocurriculum. The community ethos of the campus creates the places and spaces for faculty to have more personal interactions with students. These interactions are essentially expected of faculty and are not viewed suspiciously or as out of the norm. The community-oriented culture fosters connections between faculty and students. This is not to suggest that such a community feeling means that students are not challenged and pushed to do their best work. We found just the opposite. It is because of the community environment (read: support) that faculty are able to push students further (read: challenge).

For example, at Villanova University, campus leaders told us they are always working on breaking down the barriers between staff and faculty. For instance, in their desire for the community to be a model for students, faculty and staff are invited to campus-wide social events and forums. As the provost stated, "The students immediately see the 'collectiveness' of the campus." Based on the inspiration of St. Augustine, who stressed that one learns better in a community—one is to be surrounded by supportive friends—a sense of community is deeply embedded at Villanova. The university organizes first-year living arrangements so that students in the same residence hall take a class together in the core humanities seminar—a living and learning focus developed right from the beginning of their collegiate career.

Relative to our study, community is fostered by smaller environments where a majority of students, faculty, and staff know and tend to live in close proximity to one another. At small, tight-knit institutions, a person is not new for very long—he or she quickly becomes part of the campus community. Even at the campuses in the study that are bigger and more complex (e.g., Creighton University, University of Dayton), the concept of community is still prevalent and guarded cautiously. Part of an institution's decision to grow and evolve is how it will affect the campus community. The president of Creighton was very thoughtful in his deliberations about community:

> Our biggest challenge is to retain our size. We don't want to get much bigger but the pressure is there. There is a tension between getting bigger and losing our sense of community. Students like being on the mall and they don't want to dilute their sense of community. It's fascinating and very complimentary and very encouraging. We need to be slightly larger for our financial side, but we can't get too large or we lose the quality that we now have.

Maintaining Community Amidst Change

The campuses we studied like to think of themselves as tight-knit communities. They think deliberately and often about the challenges facing their communities. They mentioned to us that change, especially in terms of growth, has the potential to threaten the community orientation of the campus. Institutions like Creighton University are purposeful in their thinking about change and growth and how they can do so mindful of mission, size, and the ultimate effect change may have on the ethos of campus community.

Community can be taken for granted, but it is something that needs to be tended. We provide here some examples of how institutions have grappled with the changing dynamics of their campus communities. As we mentioned in Chapter 5, many faculty at Pacific Lutheran University (PLU) have moved out of neighborhoods close to campus. Historically, PLU was a place, like many of the campuses in our study, where faculty lived close to campus and students regularly moved from campus to off-campus locations. It was common for students to go to faculty homes and for faculty to be on campus in the evenings to attend student events. Shifts in faculty housing patterns have changed these social interactions. As the chair of faculty shared with us:

> Faculty live further from campus with some faculty commuting an hour a day. Some want to advise by e-mail. It's sad to see this; community is now more difficult to do. Spouses used to participate, but that's harder now. Now it seems like more of a job and [faculty] do not to go to events [as much as they used to].

The PLU community has been challenged by faculty living further from campus and from changing family patterns. Many faculty are now dual career couples, and each partner may be moving in a different career direction. Instead of living close to campus, some faculty must live in a central location to accommodate two careers. What this means is that how community used to be created (e.g., students going to faculty homes; faculty regularly attending student events) has changed. To maintain and/or recreate community calls for thinking about new ways to make it happen, and PLU has done just that. The university has helped by providing transportation to faculty homes for class dinners and by encouraging faculty to move back to campus neighborhoods through investment in these neighborhoods to make them better places to live.

Changing and evolving missions can also disrupt campus community dynamics. A recurring theme at the institutions we studied was how changing professional requirements for faculty affect campus community. Faculty and academic leaders at campuses that have raised the bar for tenure requirements (in particular increased research productivity), are concerned about the impact these new expectations will have on the local campus community and faculty connections with students (Clark, 1987). Leaders worried about limiting faculty and how changing research expectations are likely to have a ripple effect on other aspects of faculty work, including interactions with students and faculty involvement in campus service—two areas that are particularly important with regard to faculty involvement in student development. We were impressed with the time and dedication of the faculty we spoke with in our study. In addition to maintaining rigorous teaching loads (three and four classes per semester at some campuses), these faculty are also busy conducting research and writing books as well as being active in student groups and working closely with students. We found that campuses in the midst of altering things like research expectations are aware of the impact transition can have on the campus community as a whole.

Another aspect to changing and evolving missions is faculty demographics. Historically, women and racial and ethnic minorities have had a limited presence in higher education in general and at the institutions in the study in particular. Our research revealed that campuses are increasingly focused on diversifying their faculty and student bodies. However, it is still common for only one woman or racial and ethnic minority to be employed in a department. We discovered that faculty who are unique in their departments or on their campuses in terms of gender and/or race tend to be chosen more often to work with students from the same gender and/or race. The sole female faculty member in the sociology department of one of the campuses we visited talked about how the female students tend to come to her first for advising and questions they have about classes or the department. A faculty member of color in the sciences talked about his role as not so much working with minority students in his area but instead working with the college as a whole on its recruitment efforts. What we found is supported in other research about faculty (e.g., Tierney & Bensimon, 1996; Trautvetter, 1999). The important work with students is often part of the "hidden workload" of faculty (Tierney & Bensimon, 1996). Further, such involvement in service may mean faculty are challenged to contribute as much in other areas. We learned that college leaders feel this tension of evaluating faculty based on their merit and worth within the particular context of their institution.

The changing demographics of a particular campus may precipitate a reexamination of what are sometimes long-held beliefs and practices about how campuses treat their members—faculty and staff. Provosts are aware that more and more faculty are now dual career couples, which changes the dynamics of campus communities as well as faculty members when they have families. For example, when female faculty have children, this can challenge their ability to spend additional time on campus, especially for events in the evenings and on weekends (Wolf-Wendel & Ward, in press). A faculty member we spoke with who adopted a child said, "The campus helped take care of me when I adopted my baby." The community environment supported this faculty member. At the same time, dual career couples with children or single parents are more challenged to spend "endless hours" on campus with students as compared to faculty who are single, childless, or married with a spouse who does not work outside the home. More than one faculty member noted the tension between spending time with their immediate family and the "campus family." One provost stated, "Some faculty have raised their children on campus." But she noted that there has been a shift in campus community and diversity in the faculty workforce. With these changes comes a challenge to create community with diversity. The institutions expressed a desire to be open and hospitable to different ways of approaching faculty work and different types of contributions faculty make to the campus community (Bennett, 2003). But for many this is a relatively new challenge.

We offer here as a summary what we view as challenges and threats to community on campus, based on our visits. Since vibrant campus communities are instrumental to fostering the holistic development of students, these considerations (and others) are important to identify and address.

- *Faculty housing choices.* Faculty may find it challenging as a consequence of cost and character to choose housing close to campus.
- *Changes in size.* It may be challenging to maintain feelings of a close-knit community as campuses grow and enroll more students.
- *Changes in scope and/or focus.* If campuses make decisions about new areas of emphasis, campus community dynamics may be changed.
- *Faculty work.* Everyone is being asked to do more with less. Faculty who are encouraged and rewarded for their contributions are more apt to support an ethos of community on their campus.
- *Diversity.* As a campus grows and changes to accommodate more and different types of students and faculty, the ethos of community can shift. It is sometimes easier to create community amid sameness than community amid difference.

We also offer the following ideas for promoting collaborative and community-oriented environments as a way to respond to these challenges:

- *Stay mission-driven.* If a campus direction calls for faculty and staff input, have both at the table.
- *Mix committees to keep communication open.* For example, for relevant committees (e.g., academic dishonesty) have student affairs representatives on faculty committees and vice versa.
- Have the vice presidents for student affairs and academic affairs *model collaborative processes* by working together instead of at cross-purposes.

- *Hire and promote student affairs practitioners* who are cognizant of the academic affairs function, and do the same for faculty in terms of how they work with student affairs professionals.
- *Reward faculty* for their contribution to building the campus community.

Diversity Within Community

The topic of diversity within the context of campus community was a prevalent theme among the institutions in our study. More specifically, deliberate conversations regarding diversity with respect to religion, race, and geography emerged in all of our campus visits. In virtually every case, diversity dialogs of all kinds are viewed as critical to the formation and sustenance of campus environments that foster the holistic development of students. Several examples help to illustrate. First, with respect to issues of religious diversity, these campuses strive to be open and hospitable to different religious perspectives and worldviews while using their church-related legacies and identities as a backdrop and a resource for understanding. For example, at the University of Dayton, a senior faculty member has long advocated that Catholic colleges may be more successful if they focused on recruiting Catholic students from different countries, thereby providing greater exposure to diverse religions and nationalities. Diversity in terms of religion was also mentioned relative to open mindedness. Students of all faiths (not just Catholicism) at the University of Dayton are welcome to pursue their own religious beliefs as part of their holistic development while in college. For the Jewish community at Dayton, this means opportunities for students, faculty, and staff to come together to celebrate religious holidays and to discuss faith development.

Even though some of the campuses in the study are affiliated with a particular denomination or faith tradition in some manner, they still demonstrate a commitment to a variety of religious expressions. Hope College, for example, refers to itself as "reformed in tradition, but ecumenical in nature" to capture the religious character and culture of the campus. Other institutions are purposeful in bringing in external speakers to address issues associated with religious diversity. At Whitworth College, two popular professors of religious studies routinely debate issues so students can see how diversity of perspective is articulated. Faculty at Bethune-Cookman College reflect an openness to all faith traditions and foster spiritual development in students rather than promote a narrow religious orientation.

The institutions we studied also take seriously the racial diversity of their students and faculty. Each campus we visited has had some type of formalized discussion related to creating more culturally diverse campus environments. For example, the elaborate diversity plan in place at Whitworth College states,

> Our goal is for Whitworth College to be a place where the richness of an education of mind and heart is available to all people. As a Christian college, we take seriously Christ's example of loving across racial, ethnic, gender, socio-economic and religious differences.

Every unit of the campus has clearly stated its plan for diversity and the campus has had success in becoming more diverse. At Whitworth and at other campuses in the study, such a commitment is often manifest in efforts to recruit more students from diverse backgrounds and to establish better retention rates once they are there. A central part of the latter discussion, in particular, is creating campus climates that are open and welcoming to people from diverse backgrounds.

These institutions, predominantly white except for Bethune-Cookman College, find themselves challenged to diversify their campuses. Many have a severe geographic disadvantage to diversify student bodies. They have not yet determined how to go about increasing student diversity or how to effectively create a climate that supports diversity. For example, Spokane, Washington, home to Whitworth College, is a fairly homogeneous community. The college is faced with the challenge of creating campus environments for those from culturally diverse backgrounds. In contrast, campuses like Pacific Lutheran University and the University of Dayton are located in areas that are significantly more diverse and more populous. These two institutions have a larger pool of diverse populations from which to draw, and their urban settings also have more to offer in terms of community for students from diverse backgrounds. Regardless, we found that campuses are purposeful in becoming more diverse but that it can be a challenge to do so. More importantly, their efforts are not about diversity for diversity's sake. Instead their interest is driven by a commitment to take deliberate action to cultivate a campus environment that is best suited for developing students holistically (Cantor & Schomberg, 2003; Hurtado, Milem, Clayton-Pedersen, & Allen, 2000; Smith & Schonfeld, 2000). As such, the institutions in the study are interested in diversity because it contributes to the improvement of racial attitudes and also "deepens opportunities to interact with those who are different, enhances cognitive development, and results in increased overall satisfaction and involvement with the institution" (Smith & Schonfeld, 2000, p. 19). And for those with a strong religious foundation, they base the need to diversify on the principle that all people are of equal worth.

Faculty at these institutions are also committed to a diversity of viewpoints. They are acutely aware that prejudice can be subtle but strong and harmful to creating open and hospitable campus communities that nurture students' holistic development. Many faculty told us that students often come to their respective campuses set in their opinions and viewpoints and do not really want to be changed in any way by the college experience (see Chapter 4 for a larger discussion of this topic). Faculty see it as their role to provide multiple viewpoints and to expose students to different perspectives and experiences. They believe diverse campus communities provide greater opportunities for students to consider, develop and own their worldviews while thinking of themselves as part of multiple communities, not just one community.

Communities Beyond the Campus

Church-related colleges have historic missions grounded in service (Ward, 2003). These campuses were founded, in part, to prepare clergy and leadership for their particular congregations and for society in general. On the campuses that we visited, community service is alive and well. The ethic of service and community outreach was a prevalent part of student and faculty life and is intimately tied to the mission of church-related colleges to help and serve others (Heffner & Beversluis, 2002). A faculty member from Creighton University said, "We are the culture of service." The culture of service that we witnessed was manifest in two major ways: campus as neighbor and community service.

Campus as Neighbor

Ivory tower notions of higher education separate campus and community, and communities often see campuses as aloof and exclusive. Some of the metaphors we heard during our visits suggest separation between campus and community: "The ivory tower," "Up on the hill," "Behind the fence," and "Behind the pine cone curtain." As we stressed in the last section, campuses are deliberate about creating community internally. We now turn to the question—How do institutions interact with communities beyond the campus? This is a critical question because an integral part of holistic student development is not only what occurs on the physical campus, but what happens when students become involved in the external communities beyond campus.

We were impressed with the level of interaction and goodwill that existed between the institutions in the study and their respective communities. Campuses work hard at being good neighbors, and presidents, for the most part, establish the tone for neighborly interactions. Here are just a few examples:

- The president of Bethune-Cookman College holds monthly community meetings to identify community problems.
- The president of Whitworth College is active in the Spokane, Washington, community as a board member and former chair of the Chamber of Commerce.
- The president of Pacific Lutheran University has taken an active role in community development (see the following profile).
- The president of Hope College is working hard with community partners to update sports facilities.

Profile

Pacific Lutheran University

Pacific Lutheran University's (PLU) involvement in downtown redevelopment is a prime example of how a campus and community can work together and how the campus can demonstrate neighborliness. Communities adjacent to PLU have changed in character throughout the past several years, including the downtown district that is frequented by students. In the interest of keeping students close to campus, PLU has taken an active role in revitalizing downtown by engaging in real estate transactions and refurbishing properties. The area is benefiting from a neighborhood feel. Students and community members alike frequent a coffee shop and restaurants nearby. These spaces play a role in student development by simply providing places for faculty and students to congregate. According to PLU's provost, the impetus for involvement in the project "was to demonstrate PLU's continuing commitment to be 'in community' and to promote the economic well being of the local merchants, while offering the university community convenient, safe spaces to shop and gather."

Presidents lead their institutions in cultivating a sense of place that connects beyond the campus. Campuses increasingly view themselves as part of larger communities and are careful to cultivate the relationships necessary to that view. Presidents talked about the need to celebrate and to take advantage of the locations of their campuses. For example, Pacific Lutheran University is shaped by its unique northwest location; Hamline University is very much a part of Minnesota's Twin Cities community; and "Hope College *is* Holland [Michigan]," as one administrator told us. For campuses to maintain their health and vitality, they need to be concerned with the health and vitality of their local communities. The president of Creighton University equates community with "neighborliness," where the campus actively works to address issues of morality, social justice, and societal issues like education and poverty in local communities. Developing a sense of place within a community also makes student movement between campus and community more seamless.

Presidents and administrators do more than develop partnerships and community collaborations, however. Presidents play a major role in establishing connections or, as the president of Bethune-Cookman College put it, to make sure the campus is "living out the heritage." Faculty, staff, and students are also active in their communities to make them better places to live and work. For example, faculty at Union University who are involved in different community organizations take seriously their role in making Jackson, Tennessee, the best community it can be so that Union can be the best it can be. Such activity allows faculty to model the importance of community participation. Union's service to the community is highlighted in the following profile.

Profile

Union University

Part of Union University's mission statement, "Provide Christ-centered education that promotes excellence and character development in service to Church and society," is enacted in their hometown community of Jackson, Tennessee. An interesting example of student, faculty, and staff involvement in the community was described as "A Day of Remembrance." The first time this occurred, in 2003, it involved 50 service projects for 800 people. In 2004, it involved more than 60 projects and 1,000 students, faculty, and staff.

"A Day of Remembrance" was established by the university as a way to give back to the Jackson community after many individuals and businesses provided assistance when a tornado hit the campus on November 10, 2002, causing more than $2 million in damage. Classes are suspended for the day, with the exception of a few science classes, to allow students and faculty to become wholly involved in service projects. The day begins with a gathering for worship in Savage Memorial Chapel. Then students, faculty, and staff work side by side in service—sawing, hammering, planting, and working on various projects on campus and in the community. This day has become an annual event to reinforce the mission and identity of Union University.

In fall 2004, all across Jackson nearly 1,000 students, faculty, and staff took advantage of the opportunities set up by campus ministries, student life, and a group of more than 60 dedicated team leaders. Union's provost addressed those attending the opening chapel with these words: "What you do today will matter deeply to someone, even if you are working on campus." The dean of students stated, "It truly shows how leadership is being a servant." Of course, the university's hope is that service will not wait until the next "Day of Remembrance," but rather continue all year long.

Campuses also hold an important place in the community by providing a space to address current issues. For example, in anticipation of the 2004 presidential election, Union University offered one of its regular Town and Gown forums for students, faculty, and community members to learn more about the issues and the candidates. Whitworth College routinely hosts speakers on topics of current interest (e.g., gay marriage, the Iraq War) that bring in community audiences. The College of Wooster holds multiple public forums each year that address issues of public concern, drawing on nationally known speakers on current events. The forums are well attended and include a wide-ranging audience from campus and the community. These types of interactions bring the campus and community together and make for a richer learning environment for students.

Cultural events are also a common interface between campus and community. Whitworth College is host to numerous artistic and cultural events that are frequented by the community and play an important role in the arts life of the city. Similarly, sporting events at Hope College are a conduit for campus and community interactions. Institutions are good neighbors by hosting events, sharing facilities, and bringing diverse community groups to campus.

Another aspect of campus as neighbor is its relationship with local churches. An important part of holistic student development is exposure to different viewpoints and different communities. Campus leaders, especially campus ministry, noted that it is often in these different communities where students can learn from others and apply what they are learning on campus. Our research revealed that these institutions encourage students to join church communities beyond the campus. As church-related colleges, each institution in the study had places of worship on campus. Yet on Sunday mornings it is not uncommon to find these places empty because students are urged to attend church services in the community. Students are encouraged to get off campus and interact with different members of the community and see how different communities function (in this case church communities). At Hope College, there is an informal mentoring program between area church members and male students to bridge the campus with the area church communities. The program is designed for community members who want to work closely with students. This has the mutual benefit of keeping community members connected to Hope and providing opportunities for students to relate more frequently with adults in the community. Getting out into the community, meeting new people, and understanding new faith communities is viewed as an important part of the student development process. As we learned, a holistic approach to student development involves those on and off campus as well as different members of the campus community.

Community Service

Another element of campus and community interactions is community service. Church-related colleges such as those in this study have been leaders in the community service movement popular in higher education today (Heffner & Beversluis, 2002; Ward, 2003). Part of being a community member is working actively to solve the problems facing the community. Through their faculty, students, and staff, college campuses play a key role in providing these services.

The contribution students make to local communities through service is significant, according to both faculty and professionals in student affairs. For example, at Creighton University, 100 % of medical school students are involved in service that provides a great incentive to undergraduates to get involved; each year 700 Villanova University students go on service trips; Union University hosts an annual community day; and at Bethune-Cookman College, all first-year students engage in a community project as a part of their freshman-year experience.

We noted the breadth of opportunities that faculty, staff, and students engage in as part of the service culture on these campuses. These types of service fall into the following areas:

- *Service-learning:* Community service components as part of the formal curriculum
- *Volunteerism:* Service that is done beyond the curriculum (also called community service)
- *Immersion trips:* Extended periods of service sometimes involving a faculty member and a curricular component
- *Spring break trips* related to service
- *Weekend involvement* in service (e.g., "urban plunge" at the University of Dayton)

We highlight these different types of service because some of them are closely tied to the curriculum and are deliberately part of the teaching and learning process (see Chapter 4). Others are planned and structured as a complement to the curriculum but are still an important part of holistic student development.

We found that colleges are with a variety of service affiliations and partnerships with the community. For example, during

Bethune-Cookman College's monthly meetings with the community, the president discusses and takes action related to problems facing the community. The campus is a significant partner in needs assessment and community service; there is a broad base of involvement. At other campuses, community service is more localized or project oriented, using a methodical way to alert the campus to the particular issues facing the community and the opportunities for service that exist. Campuses that have established offices of community service have more deliberate and purposeful interactions with communities. For example, the Raymond L. Fitz, S. M. Center for Leadership in Community was established at the University of Dayton to develop partnerships with urban communities to enhance community building and to provide a context for "connected learning and scholarship."

Based on our campus visits, multiple communities are the focus of community service projects. On some campuses the focus was largely on the local community whereas others had a significant sense of global communities. On every campus, students had ample opportunity to participate in international experiences, and many of them were required to complete a service component. These experiences tend to be life-transforming events and are an important part of student development. Most service experiences, and in particular those in global contexts, take students out of their daily routine and challenge them to think about their place in the world. Students may go on these experiences planning to get exposure to international perspectives, but they tend to come back with a far greater sense of who they are and how they fit in the world.

Service, regardless of the type, helps students to get off campus and "out of their comfort zone." At Whitworth College, a professor told us that he saw students "taking risks through service." A Pacific Lutheran University student shared with us that her study abroad experience included a service-learning component and put her in close proximity to the professor who led to the trip. The experience was an event that stands out as most important in the college education process.

Service also develops a sense of vocation in students. As students think about who they are, how they want to live their lives, and what they are called to do (i.e., vocation), involvement in the community can help clarify purpose in life, according to campus leaders. Service provides opportunities for students to get outside of themselves and to serve others. Service is also an opportunity for students to integrate their learning and development and an ethic of care. At the campuses in the study, service was talked about in civic terms (e.g., community service) and also in more religious terms (e.g., serving others out of a sense of gratitude and an obligation to use their gifts and talents to benefit others). These conceptions of service shape student involvement in the community and how students see themselves as community members.

Service also allows students to give back to their communities in terms of place (e.g., Daytona Beach) and culture (e.g., African-American community). At Bethune-Cookman College, service is not only about "helping," "doing good," and refining career choices (though all these things undoubtedly take place), it is also about giving back to the people and to one's community. Students at Bethune-Cookman are urged to recognize that if it were not for those who have preceded them (family, friends, community members), it would not be possible even to be in college. Service is a way to honor and give back to those who have gone before them. Special focus colleges, such as Bethune-Cookman, a Historically Black College, are unique in encouraging this aspect of service (Ayers & Ray, 1996; Ward, 2003; Ward & Wolf-Wendel, 2000). The president of Bethune-Cookman put it this way:

> They [students] need to do a minimum number hours in the community—to give back to society, especially their people. We tell students they are

> fortunate to be here in college. The point is to be a responsible citizen. There is an obligation to share our wealth.

Such a view challenges students to think about their place in their communities and the role of a college education in preparing one for life and service to others (see the profile of Bethune-Cookman College in Chapter 3).

We were impressed with the pervasiveness of service on some campuses. For example, The College of Wooster has established the Wooster Volunteer Network, which provides activities that range from assisting a local nursing home to mentoring seventh-grade students. Service is infused throughout the curriculum and cocurriculum. The Wooster Volunteer Network also extends to alumni in their respective cities across the nation every year on the same weekend. At Villanova University, service is pervasive and has a very close tie to the Augustinian mission of the campus. The president talks about service as a way to educate students in faith and action.

Community service is related to faculty involvement in holistic student development in some of the following ways:

- Faculty and students engage in service together. Such immersion experiences break down barriers between students and faculty.
- Student service experiences enter into classroom discussions and shape interactions with faculty.
- Service in the context of the church-related college can be motivated by students' ethic of service shaped by their church and/or faith. Such involvement can lead to questions of faith, learning, and vocation. Faculty are often part of these conversations.
- Student involvement in service experiences can shape what they want to do with their careers and where they want to

do it. Faculty can be part of the interaction and part of helping students decipher their vocation.

Dealing With Difference and External Communities

Given the homogeneity of these campuses, the surrounding community, which in many cases is more diverse than the campus, presents a challenge and an opportunity for students to gain experience with diversity. It also challenges students to think about their orientation to service in ways that go beyond a perspective of helping and charity to one of change (Heffner & Beversluis, 2002; Morton, 1995). For example, the orientation of some campuses had a strong focus on social justice and societal change. Thus, these colleges are intent for students to go into external communities and to gain opportunities with diverse populations.

The community service center at Creighton University provides a good example of preparing students for work in diverse communities. All service experiences are accompanied by training and reflection programs, and it is not surprising that campuses in more urban areas (Hamline University, University of Dayton, Villanova University, Pacific Lutheran University, Creighton University) have more highly evolved programs to deal with the complexity of race. Campus leaders know that they have a great opportunity to work "in their own backyards" (i.e., their own local communities) to recruit more diverse student bodies. For example, as communities like Dayton, Omaha, and St. Paul have become more diverse, the universities of Dayton, Creighton, and Hamline have found increased and unique opportunities to become more diverse on campus as well as more thoughtful in their interactions with off-campus communities. Creighton, for example, has one of the largest Native American student bodies as the result of recruiting efforts among this population in their region.

The following are some suggestions for implementing service activities, based on our findings:

- Service experiences that partner staff, faculty, and students impact each party. In particular, they help promote faculty involvement in student development experiences that bring different campus constituents together.
- Service without reflection can perpetuate stereotypes.
- Partnering students new to service with those who are experienced in particular placements helps smooth transitions into service experiences and can provide a source of reflection.
- Thorough and extended involvement in off-campus activities and immersion experiences is more likely to impact students and increase the interactions they have with faculty during these experiences.

Summary

Campus community is about creating communities that are open, welcome, and caring of all members. It also means engaging with communities beyond the campus. In light of the diversity of religion, race, gender, and thought that is present within the institutions in our study, we found that campuses were thoughtful in how they cultivate community and external community relations. In particular, we highlight the following points to summarize what we found about campus community and relationships with communities beyond the campus:

- Shared governance—involving all members of the community in deciding on its priorities—includes all members of the campus community in decision-making and in creating community.

- Diversity on campus is valued and institutions in the study purposefully includc multiple and diverse people and viewpoints.
- Colleges are active as community citizens in the larger society, with faculty, staff, administrators, and students all playing a part.
- Community service is broadly defined and provides multiple opportunities for involvement. Students can participate in the community through the curriculum (e.g., service learning) and through cocurricular experiences (e.g., spring break trips).

Questions for Campus Conversations

- *How is community talked about at your institution? Does it refer to specific relationships and patterns of behavior among faculty, students, and staff?*
- *What can you and your colleagues do to cultivate an even greater sense of campus community?*
- *How does your campus community reflect your campus culture—your identity and character as an institution? Does the culture of the campus support your specific ethos of community?*
- *What does shared governance mean at your institution? Who has major and minor voices in your community?*
- *How does your institution define diversity? How does it maintain unity within diversity?*
- *How do you view the campus community in its relationships with communities beyond the campus?*
- *What do you currently do to cultivate an ethic of service and care? How do you encourage students to enter into service experiences with an orientation toward social change?*
- *What contributions are expected of faculty? Does your institution reward faculty for fulfilling these expectations, such as participation in governance and involvement in the community?*

7 Creating Communities That Put Students First

"We encourage students to let their intellectual life be guided by their hearts. Students are learning and developing in college for a purpose; that is, to be of service to the world."

—Provost, Villanova University

Introduction

Throughout this book we have highlighted institutions that foster holistic student development. We have argued that students do not develop and learn in a vacuum. Rather, they develop patterns of behavior that grow out of their own sense of self and that are influenced by their campus environments. In turn, students are investing their time and talents in activities that bring them meaning and purpose, and it is hoped that students will continue to contribute to the larger society as they live out their lives. The institutions we studied are promoting approaches that engage students in meaningful activities and experiences, but we have also noted the many tensions and challenges facing colleges and universities as they undertake these efforts. With this as the context, we now summarize the findings from our visits to these 10 institutions and present some calls for consideration and action that we hope will illuminate the tasks and challenges ahead of the larger academy as it tries to develop students holistically.

From our sample of institutions, we have learned much about how faculty and professional staff organize their collegiate environments. They have an eye on desired ends—what they want students to be and to become, and to what end students invest their time, talents, and energies. These college leaders—faculty and administration—also have asked and intentionally tried to foster holistic student development—individually and collectively as a community.

More specifically, these colleges focus on nurturing students' sense of self, including purpose in life, and their involvement and engagement; they emphasize the importance of both being and doing.

In the preceding chapters, we used the 4C framework—culture, curriculum, cocurriculum, and community—to describe how these colleges plan, organize, and implement their sociocultural environments to foster student development effectively. For each of the Cs, we have summarized how college leaders and faculty address the challenge of implementing student development with a holistic view. We have focused on how these colleges intentionally develop students holistically, particularly how faculty contribute to the education of the students both inside and outside of the classroom. We tried to portray how faculty and their colleagues think, plan, create, and sustain a campus community that focuses on the interior lives of students—values, spirituality, identity, purpose, and meaning—as well as their exterior lives—their observable patterns of behavior. We used Personal Investment Theory to guide us in describing and explaining an integrated way to view students' development because it emphasizes the inextricable connections among students' behaviors, their sense of self, and the campus environment.

We selected 10 church-related colleges that we consider to be individually and collectively distinguished and distinctive in fostering holistic student development. As we noted, not all of the colleges have the same mission or identity. For example, they differ significantly on how they wish to assist students regarding faith development. Some do so in the context of evangelical Christianity, whereas others desire their students to be liberally educated and to find meaning in life with or without a specific religious commitment or perspective. We support this diversity since a strength of the American higher education system is its highly disparate institutions, even among the colleges that were founded by a church denomination.

Despite these differences among the institutions we studied, we have focused largely on their commonalities. More specifically, these colleges share two characteristics in common: they desire to foster students' holistic development, and they have a legacy in a faith tradition that makes faith development an important part of holistic student development. These commonalities are important characteristics of American higher education and have wide applicability for any college or university that is engaged in undergraduate education. At the same time, our interest is not to advocate an "ideal college" or a monolithic portrayal of a church-related college. We are not arguing that these colleges are model institutions, or have a set of best practices, or are to be emulated. Rather we are hoping that leaders of any college interested in student development will consider ways to generate similar results and perspectives on their own campuses.

We have organized our findings in the form of three major characteristics that any college or university should consider if its educational leaders wish to significantly involve faculty in developing students holistically. These three characteristics are:

- Mission is reality, not rhetoric.
- Learning and development are integrated.
- The campus community fosters support and challenge.

Each characteristic encompasses all the dimensions of culture, curriculum, cocurriculum, and community in and beyond the campus—the 4Cs. We also realize that no one C can be addressed without consideration of the other Cs. Integration is very important in fostering holistic student development, and so we also have had to think in an integrative way to illustrate how the 4Cs collectively play themselves out in a college setting.

Each characteristic is summarized based on our findings from the 10 colleges. The summaries are not meant to represent a set of criteria of excellence. They are meant to be descriptive rather than normative. The calls for consideration and action we present should be interpreted as issues to be addressed, polices to consider, points for campus conversations, challenges to be overcome, and opportunities to discuss possible strategies, policies, and practices on local campuses interested in fostering holistic student development. We end our discussion of each of the three major characteristics with a set of questions designed to spark conversations within campus communities.

Mission Is Reality, Not Rhetoric

At the institutions we visited, a mission statement is more than a line in a catalog or in the minutes of a board meeting. Rather, the mission is rooted in the college's tradition and continuously guides the campus community in its sense of direction. It is alive, working, and evolving. Institutions that effectively foster holistic student development are clear about their mission and the campus community believes in and rallies around the mission. At these colleges, legacy forms the foundation of mission and identity; mission and identity drive expectations, standards of excellence, and modes of operation; leadership is critical to advancing the mission and identity of the college; and the campus as a community "polishes rather than varnishes."

The church-related legacies of the colleges we studied most assuredly have changed since these institutions were founded. However, one way they continue to clearly express their legacies is how they position themselves in the larger society. These colleges encourage students to engage with society, but to some desired end, often going beyond what current society deems important. They each espouse an image of the "good life," which is more often defined more as a "life worth living is an examined one" rather than in terms of "worldly success." At these colleges the ultimate criterion of a quality and effective college preparation is not personal gain per se, but guiding students to lead meaningful lives that often include being active in society to help improve it. To be sure, some of the colleges are more explicit than others in using a religious worldview or perspective in their desire to assist students in this effort. It is important to stress that each college defines and interprets the good life differently, based on its own traditions, legacy, commitments, and convictions. But all colleges strive intentionally to develop students to become "good persons" who will engage all of life from some principled perspective. In essence, they are following Aristotle's lead in believing a good community provides the environment in which everyone has an opportunity to realize his or her personal excellence.

The colleges in this study place their mission and identity at the forefront of their visioning, planning, and implementation. They sense they are on a journey, with their mission as their guide. They desire to make their mission larger than life in many ways—a transcendent quality that drives, motivates, and gives meaning to their venture individually and collectively as a college community. They all continuously discuss, debate, and vote on their mission, often using it as the cornerstone of the strategic planning process, including curricular revisions. They use their mission to establish priorities such as their emphasis on fostering a holistic education for undergraduates; selection of degree programs; recognition of faculty contributions in mentoring students, leadership within the college community, and research; and building community to foster student, faculty, and staff development.

Leadership at these colleges is critical in creating purposeful campus cultures. Presidents are the conveners for continuous conversations about the mission and identity of the college, and they serve as the primary communicators of the mission. Leaders, such as presidents and provosts, serve as gatekeepers of the mission and identity of the college. For example, without their support and insistence on a faith or religious perspective, the college community would likely drift toward a posture where faith and learning are not well integrated. Strong leaders take advantage of all possible opportunities (e.g., convocations, graduations, forums, roundtables) to articulate the mission to the campus community. Communication is wide, continuous, and consistent. We discovered that college administrators stay "on message," always finding an opportunity to remind people of how a particular goal or initiative relates to the institutional mission.

Leaders work on empowering the entire campus community to take ownership of the mission. In particular, they recognize that faculty are the primary group who keep the mission alive on a daily basis, inside and outside of the classroom. "Faculty members, as they will frequently remind administrators, are not just employees of the institution; a college's faculty is the college" (Kennedy & Simon, 2005, p. 227).

The colleges fulfill their mission and identity by continuously polishing rather than varnishing. The entire community polishes to reveal the core, keep, or restore the essence of what it is to be. They know the core has a centeredness and a rootedness. They work from a deep internalized commitment to maintain the core identity and character of what is being polished and have pride in the process and the product. Their task of polishing is internally motivated, and their "being" generates and drives their "doing," which in turn is mutually reinforcing.

Likewise, campus leaders avoid varnishing—covering over or sealing their work from the outside. They do not work to get the task of creating a community done quickly. Their aim is not to make the campus appear glossy by covering up the rough edges. They do not reject feedback or avoid being responsive to those on the outside. Instead, they listen for ways to improve, knowing that the image is not as important as the substance. They are in it for the long haul, viewing the process of polishing as a challenge filled with hard, diligent work but one that leads to integrity, authenticity, and fulfillment.

Calls for Consideration and Action

Invoke mission as a sense of purpose.

Regard the college's mission as a pervasive call to action. Leaders, staff, and faculty can view the college's mission with a sense of duty and reverence, using it as a guide and rationale to get everyone engaged and involved. It can be used to help the community make adjustments and to prevent them from being too responsive to the fads of the day and time; it helps a college to stay the course. As we learned, the mission serves as an anchor in times of expansion and prosperity but also in times of challenge. Treating the mission as having an almost transcendent quality, even bigger than life, is what many of these colleges seemed to be doing and it gives them a sense of excitement and determination. Invoking mission is about the campus staying purposeful about its mission.

Use the mission to determine college priorities.

Employ the mission and identity of a college as the basis for establishing priorities. The mission is what a college can effectively use in selecting its learning and development goals and its priorities. As we learned, aligning the mission with actual priorities allows the community members to quickly learn what really counts. Mission linked to allocation of funds and rewarding faculty and staff is critical, according to our study.

The pressure to do excellent professional work is always present among the faculty in these institutions—a universal feeling in higher education. Colleges interested in fostering civic, moral, and faith development, as well as intellectual and social development, are aware they cannot only be competitive within the larger academy in educating their students. Maintaining mission commitments and conforming to the hegemonic influences of the larger academy, at times, may be a source of tension. If these institutions face these two challenges well, however, they may be able to be more influential and distinguished in both transforming students and playing a transformative role in society.

Think value added based on mission.

Use assessment to help leaders and faculty better understand the mission and its fulfillment. Assessment can be a major strategy and mechanism for faculty and staff to understand connections between the ends and the means. They can focus on such questions as—Why are students developing in certain ways during their college years? To what extent is student growth and development influenced by their enrollment at a given college or in a program? What curricular and cocurricular programs are particularly influential? What experiences have the most and least impact on students?

Campus leaders and faculty can consider the notion of value added in addressing these kinds of questions, asking about the impact on student development that can be reasonably attributed to attendance and participation in a given college or program. For leaders and faculty, value added can be as much a frame of mind as a practical blueprint for a specific assessment strategy. It can help leaders select what characteristics, abilities, values, and patterns of student behavior are to be highlighted, emphasized, and intentionally selected for development. And it helps leaders and faculty select which curricular and cocurricular activities appear to have the most promise for impact.

As we learned in our study, many faculty already think and talk in terms of students' holistic development during college and what they consider to be among the "causes" of such growth. They have acquired considerable experiential knowledge about student learning and development. If they are also systematic in their descriptions and monitoring, they can offer valuable input for thought, reflection, and analysis in discussions among the major stakeholders on campus.

Link leadership with ownership.
Think of leadership as encompassing all members of the community—students, faculty, staff. All can be empowered to assist others in their development. We learned that students view faculty and staff as role models, and they accept this responsibility with a great deal of seriousness. But they also know how important it is to empower students to lead. We learned that one of the most effective strategies at these colleges was to have all members take ownership of the mission, each having distinctive roles in carrying it out. Formal authority per se is not the distinguishing characteristic but rather the extent of active participation and ownership of the campus's mission and programs. Students especially benefit since they are already learning the challenges of leading as well as following. They can get opportunities to lead from their sense of purpose and mission.

Questions for Campus Conversations

- *How does the mission statement of your institution reflect the legacy, current identity and character, and vision for the future of your campus?*
- *How does your institution's mission determine curricular and cocurricular priorities?*
- *To what extent is the campus community—faculty, students, and staff—committed to the institution's mission and identity? To communities beyond the campus?*
- *Who do you consider to be the champions or leaders of holistic student development?*
- *How do you know you are effectively investing in your students to develop holistically?*

Learning and Development Are Integrated

Holistic student development calls for viewing the college experience as fostering both learning and development. The colleges in our study desire to develop students to engage in critical thinking, grow in their social and ethical responsibility, develop skills for careers and for living, and gain an integrated sense of self. They also want to guide students in their faith development, defined in terms of making meaning in one's life. They support Boyer's (1987) desired goal of a college education:

> We need educated men and women who not only pursue their own personal interests but are also prepared to fulfill their social and civic obligations. And it is during the undergraduate experience, perhaps more than at any other time, that these essential qualities of mind and character are refined. (p. 7)

These colleges purposefully create environments that are committed to nurturing the heart as well as developing the mind. They are continuously trying to connect intellectual and moral purpose (Hatch, 2005). In doing so, they are assisting students with their vocation in life, challenging them with developing their vision of and commitment to a good life, which often includes but is not fully defined in terms of a successful career. They are intent in preparing students to be competitive in the world, educating them to be productive workers in the labor force, and to contribute to society as good citizens.

But it is faculty and staff involvement in assisting students to find purpose and meaning in their lives that makes these colleges particularly distinctive. They view learning and development as integrated and holistic, with a focus on self-understanding and service to others. All of the colleges in the study underscore this view, though each may have a particular end in mind for such learning and/or differ with respect to how they attempt to cultivate it (e.g., colleges that operate within a particularly prominent Christian worldview may frame the goal and process of holistic student development differently than an institution that undertakes this work based on a different starting point). Independent of the explicit nature of an institution's religious affiliation and mission, however, faculty and administrators at the colleges in the study generally tended to view faith development as a rigorous, intellectual challenge in which the head and the heart are integrated in the search for truth, meaning, and fulfillment. Faith and learning are not two separate spheres in the life of students and faculty, divided into the private and the public, but rather they are connected and integrated to foster wholeness.

Faculty are expected to be and are highly involved in assisting students in character and faith development, admittedly difficult and demanding work as many faculty noted during the interviews. These faculty-student relationships significantly help students to better understand their notions of vocation, sense of self, perspectives on life, and career aspirations. In the office hours, immersion trips, science labs, music rehearsals, social events, and visits to the homes of faculty and staff, the more personal issues and questions of meaning and life are often addressed. For both students and faculty, there are appropriate times and places for such interactions to occur, especially in the area of faith development.

Many faculty see themselves as models to students in integrating faith and learning. The manner of their modeling varies considerably from college to college and among faculty at a particular college. Not all desire to reveal their faith inside or outside of the classroom. All faculty and professionals, however, agree that the most effective way to influence and guide students in their development—whether it be primarily an intellectual focus or deeply involving one's personal values and faith commitment—is to "walk the talk." At all colleges, faculty and their colleagues are encouraged to be themselves so the college can have as many models as there are persons. But the social pressures and the visibility of everyone on a relatively small campus—one of the strengths of these colleges—can sometimes present a challenge for faculty, staff, and students to be themselves. Some question how honest they can or wish to be about issues of personal values, national policy, family, and church dogma. Academic leaders and faculty all agree that this is an individual matter to be handled with caution and care.

Calls for Consideration and Action

Create the curriculum to foster holistic student development rather than an accumulation of academic credits.

Consider the curriculum as a primary means to help students better understand themselves and the world around them. As we learned, everyone regards critical self-reflection as necessary to holistic development. In doing so, faculty learn that understanding the level of intellectual and emotional maturity and complexity of the students as they enter and progress through college is essential to their teaching and working with students. Based on our study, faculty and professional staff learn much from each other and can effectively assist each other in becoming more aware and knowledgeable about student readiness to change and grow and in designing activities that address this readiness.

The institutions we studied try to align their pedagogy to reflect the mission of the college. Faculty members deliberately employ a variety of pedagogical strategies in the classroom to provide students with multiple perspectives and to deepen their understanding of their own worldviews and perspectives. For example, the senior-year experience—a capstone course—is often used to help students integrate faith, academic understanding, and interests.

Acknowledge the risks of assisting and guiding students to integrate their learning and faith.

Recognize that relationships between students and faculty become more complex, difficult, and controversial when faculty are involved in fostering character, faith, and spiritual development of students. Some faculty may desire to avoid being engaged in fostering moral and faith development of students, but in doing so they may not be taking advantage of the students' goals to develop in personal ways. Involvement is a better option if openness and respect for all perspectives is a part of student-faculty relationships (Connor, 2005). Almost all faculty agree that they need to be actively and intentionally engaged if they wish to assist in developing students holistically. "Effective faculty take an interest in students and learn from the students what the main questions are. We need to know who the student is. We cannot touch the hearts of students unless we know them," observed a vice president for student affairs. They also recognize that doing so requires considerable time together, since faculty and students need to get to know each other in order to establish trust. This type of engagement inevitably leads to vulnerability and can sometimes result in the parties knowing each other too well. Some noted that being a teacher is not the same as being a pastor or personal counselor. Thus determining boundaries is one of the most important issues a college community faces when faculty and staff deliberately become mentors to students.

The leaders and faculty we talked to recognize that this integration comes from active engagement with those with differing points of view and perspectives. One needs to go beyond mere tolerance, to make attempts to understand others and seek out understanding and shared values for the common good, with a recognition and acceptance of differences (Nash, 2001). Practicing hospitality is needed (Bennett, 2003), and faculty and staff play an important role as a strong intellectual and adult presence to students. In general, faculty prefer not to see students float and drift through college. As one senior faculty member stated, "Being rooted is not the same as being buried in a tradition." They are willing to accept the role that students need models to watch, and they recognize that students are watching, which was confirmed often by the students we interviewed.

When faculty accept a responsibility to assist students in their holistic development, they assume the role of moral educators. They are, in essence, becoming *in loco amicis*—"wise friends"—to students (Willimon & Naylor, 1995). In doing so, they become keenly aware that students are growing and developing from their past—a very personal journey. Students do not leave their goals and sense of self at the campus gate when they enter college. As students develop a life of commitment and conviction—a life of purpose—they are engaged in more than knowledge acquisition. Holistic development is not a simple pattern of change; thus the settings for faith and moral development are not limited to the formal classroom setting (Wellman, 2003). It best occurs when a faculty member can be viewed by students and colleagues as "professor as person," as we discussed earlier in the book.

Blend organizational distinctions among academic affairs, students affairs, and ministry.

Examine the organizational structures in terms of mission fulfillment, which stresses integration of student experiences. In our study we were impressed with the frequency that faculty and staff keep the question "What is best for the students?" at the forefront of their planning and implementation. Colleges continuously look for ways to break down barriers to create a seamless educational environment. One common strategy for consideration is creating reporting lines that connect academic affairs and student affairs (e.g., the director of freshman programs reporting to both the provost and vice president for student affairs, or the dean of students reporting to the provost).

The colleges in the study implicitly, if not explicitly, honored the notion of seamless integration—students develop holistically and who they are and what they do are highly integrated. Thus all members generally supported the college's attempt to think, plan, and implement holistically, although not everyone, particularly faculty, desired to be personally involved. At these institutions, the student affairs and ministry professionals want to more closely align with faculty, not unlike the national trend (American College Personnel Association & National Association of Student Personnel Administrators, 2004; Brown, 1996).

Many leaders have stressed the importance of integration and wholeness of the campus, believing that "It takes a whole campus to educate the whole student." Father Charles Currie (2005) argues that Jesuit colleges and universities have always had as their goal to be "total care institutions" (p. 1), creating "seamless" experiences for students, with student affairs professionals collaborating with faculty and campus ministry. He does, however, point out that this integration is not without its challenges.

Create a curriculum and cocurriculum that jointly highlights both learning and development.

Consider student engagement as both an end and a means. The mere experience of witnessing events, visiting different cultures, and meeting and knowing people from different cultural and ethnic backgrounds is good in and of itself, according to many we spoke with. Student engagement brings richness and diversity to one's development and fosters desirable strengths (Kuh, Kinzie, Schuh, Whitt, & Associates, 2005).

Moreover, we learned that these colleges do not view engagement and involvement independent of reflection and critical self-discovery. Engagement is more effective and lasting if accompanied by reflection and analysis (Shulman, 2002). Colleges have realized that some strategies are more effective in developing students to better understand and internalize their commitments and convictions. At times we heard faculty discussing this in terms of a student's journey of faith development, in which he or she arrives on campus with a rather rigid way of viewing reality and becomes more able and willing to reflect on alternative views and perspectives.

These colleges offer courses or provide noncredit opportunities to help students learn more about themselves in relation to their lives and career goals. Some offer first-year courses that integrate career counseling with vocation and personal development. Some require campus-wide capstone experiences to help students integrate what they have learned in previous courses for application to key social and value-laden problems and issues and in their personal lives. Discussions about how the curriculum might advance students toward greater intellectual and moral complexity are important according to faculty in the study.

Questions for Campus Conversations

- *What are your specific goals for holistic student learning and development? How are they expressed?*
- *What are the key issues your institution needs to address in order to design curricular and cocurricular programs that foster holistic student development?*
- *What role does faith development play in your efforts to develop students holistically?*
- *What pedagogical strategies do you consider to be the most effective in guiding and assisting students in their self-identity, including a sense of purpose, vocation, and career preparation?*
- *How do faculty and staff collaborate at your institution to develop students holistically?*

- *What is the common understanding of faculty and staff at your institution in regard to serving as campus role models to guide students in their moral, civic, and faith development?*

The Campus Community Fosters Support and Challenge

Fostering holistic student development requires both support and challenge. The colleges in the study rely heavily on community to fulfill their goals and mission. They recognize that students (and faculty and staff) best develop their identity in community with others, within a safe environment where they question, test boundaries, and refine their identity. Leaders and faculty make a concerted effort to respect the personhood of everyone, simultaneously advocating unity of purpose and diversity of viewpoints, perspectives, and people.

The notion of community is very strong at these colleges. Community is important because it provides comfort and support when sadness, failures, and tragedies occur in life. Somewhat paradoxically, these colleges develop a community of hope, often based on their religious convictions. They have a desire to help students understand and give them perspectives to find meaning in a world that often lacks meaning (Gomes, 2002). Thus they create communities that are caring and concerned with the whole person, including the affective and spiritual dimensions of students' lives.

Colleges desire to promote pluralism and unity respectively. The deans and provosts we interviewed stressed the importance of their colleges having a strong and effectively communicated sense of purpose, but also respecting and encouraging the diversity of values and personal faith traditions of students, faculty, and staff. Academic leaders expect faculty to be free to express their personal perspectives when and where appropriate given their mission and culture, but not to force them on others. Sensitivity is required, as is the fundamental principle of respecting and celebrating differences. For many, it means not sharing one's values or faith and religious perspectives with others. Faculty sharing their personal perspectives to faculty colleagues is also not the same as sharing personal beliefs and values with students. Many of the academic leaders interviewed noted the potential danger of faculty and staff being too influential to students on personal matters.

Appropriate relationships between faculty and colleagues, especially with students, is a controversial topic and one on which faculty and leaders have definite opinions. Should a faculty member's religion, faith, personal values, and commitments influence his or her teaching and scholarship? No one argues that faculty can be totally value free or completely objective in their work. They deal with questions like—What exactly do and can faculty share with students? How and when do they share? For some faculty, integrating faith with reason and learning is expected, natural, and essential, and they are comfortable discussing the connections. For others, it is considered too personal or inappropriate. Still others differentiate between assisting students in their civic and moral development and guiding them in their faith and spiritual quest.

Calls for Consideration and Action

Develop a creative tension between challenge and support. Create a community that is both challenging and supportive. These colleges view their campuses as a "mentoring community," where faculty are the key players often working collaboratively with others in student affairs and ministry to develop students. "At its best, higher education is distinctive in its capacity to serve as a mentoring environment in the formation of critical adult faith" (Parks, 2000, p. 159). They understand the challenge of accepting students where they are, which means they need to work with students who often see the world in stark black and white terms and are vulnerable at this stage of their lives. Faculty and professionals understand that they can best guide them not by tearing apart their worlds and perspectives on life, including their faith and religious backgrounds, without a plan of reconstruction. They are committed to assisting students by questioning, challenging, and supporting. The approach often described to us reminds us of the notion of "flow" developed by Csikszentmihalyi (1997). We were impressed with how some faculty are able to balance support and challenge, taking into account the developmental stage of students and encouraging them to move beyond their current level of sophistication. As many told us, this is very difficult work.

Support and challenge is a collective responsibility. As some faculty mentioned, a false dichotomy is created when support and challenge are structured in terms of faculty challenging and student affairs professionals supporting. We learned that students are best guided in their development when everyone is challenging *and* supportive.

Consider community and diversity as complementary. Consider community and diversity as complementary, not contradictory of each other. As we learned, both community and diversity are needed to assist students in developing their faith and purpose in life. Diversity within the academy or on a college campus is needed to stimulate students to think and explore. It prevents indoctrination, according to the faculty. "The genius of [our college] is that there are as many models as there are molds." This comment by a faculty member conveys how colleges design the environment to incorporate diversity on their campuses. Diversity is important because it gives students opportunities to watch and learn that authority figures can in fact disagree on very important issues.

Community is also critical because it allows for diversity to exist and flourish on a campus. Community—a set of shared values and commitments to something beyond each individual—prevents isolation and extreme relativism. Community lessens the possibility of everyone talking past each other, which does not allow for integration to occur. Thus it is this tension between advocating diversity and community around a set of shared values that makes a college vibrant and creative. It makes possible communication, conversation, and exploration among its members, and it provides some necessary boundaries to search for defensible understandings and truths. Community allows and encourages students to take risks, support each other, and develop commitments to take action. Community, when open and hospitable, is more than a place for "values clarification"; it is a place for students to develop their commitments and begin to act on them (Mannoia, 2000).

Create an environment that fosters critical and constructive thinking and doing.

Create a campus culture and community that encourages students to be critical and constructive thinkers and doers. The institutions we studied ask the following questions: Is our mission and are our programs designed and implemented to develop students to be critical thinkers and committed to addressing real-world problems? Are we preparing students to "make a difference"? Many leaders seek answers to these questions by connecting faith with learning and learning with living (Mannoia, 2000).

According to Shulman (2004), the academy has two major functions in assisting students to develop as human beings. First, the academy honors and promotes skepticism, disbelief, and finding fault in the current understanding of a topic or issue. It is dedicated to the self-correction of knowledge, regardless of its source of knowing. In short, it is to be a critical place—a community of criticism. But that is only half of the acadamy's responsibility. It is also a place where scholars—teachers and students alike—try to make sense of the world, to take chaos and order it. Thus the academy goes beyond analysis and critique to engage in synthesis and the creation of worldviews as viable interpretations and perspectives. It is "dangerous" work, since the goals of building and constructing are very difficult and can lead to false truths about how we can and should live. It is a function for which the academy can greatly contribute to student development.

This theme of integration is also important in how colleges view professional education. They are advocates of preparing students for a profession, but they also desire to provide students with a values-based education. As one provost told us, "We do not want to just educate students to get the train there on time, but want them to also consider and question where the train is going." A good education can be judged by its usefulness and instrumentality, but the criterion is not limited to career preparation alone. The value of a good education is to be couched within the definition of the "good life." Thus an education is useful and effective to the extent to which it addresses the major issues of finding vocation—Who am I? How can I best contribute to the world in which I now live? In short, a good education has both intrinsic and instrumental value to each of these colleges.

Create a community of support and challenge for all members. Putting students first does not mean that the other members of the campus community—faculty, staff, administrators—should be neglected. All need to be supported and challenged for a vibrant community to exist. Since faculty and staff are at different stages of their professional and personal lives, it is important to view their development as a lifelong journey. As we learned in this study, faculty development properly begins with recruitment and orientation and continues throughout the life of the faculty member. A strong and purposeful faculty development program helps faculty grow and develop in both their professional and personal lives. The goal is to help faculty and staff think of their careers as a very important part of vocation (Haughey, 2004). It is this distinction between career and calling that is critical for faculty and staff serving as models and mentors to students. Students are able to see that each faculty and staff member is supported as a "whole person"—just as they themselves are supported.

These colleges take into account two major dimensions of congruence. First, how do faculty and staff see their careers as reflecting a sense of self, sense of purpose, and vocation? Does their work reflect who they are? Are they able to be personally invested, acting out of their convictions and identities. Ideally, faculty and staff can view their lives as purposeful, integrating personal and professional goals and aims. These communities know the importance of career being a part of one's vocation, since it is a powerful factor in motivation, satisfaction, and commitment.

Second, how do faculty and staff consider their place of work as supportive of their goals and contributions? Do they feel at home at this college? We like the notion of *readiness* rather than the words *fit* or *match*. A faculty member may not completely fit or match the existing community as defined by its current set of values, norms, and expectations of behavior. But this provides a challenge for the community to be hospitable (Bennett, 2003), and it allows for new members of the community to make a difference.

By paying attention to these two congruencies, colleges can assist faculty and staff to feel fulfilled and motivated when both sets of congruencies exist. Being personally invested means one is acting on his or her sense of purpose and finds meaning in investing his or her time and talents, ideally in ways that are aligned with the college's mission and vision (Braskamp & Hager, 2005; Lindholm, 2003; Maehr & Braskamp, 1986). This perspective is viewed by campus leaders as critical to helping students develop holistically. Students are able to witness firsthand how others integrate their personal and professional lives, even when this integration comes with some difficulty. They can see the power of challenge and support in the lives of their mentors.

Support and reward faculty and staff for their contributions to the community.

Examine evaluation policies and practices in light of the college's mission and vision. Are faculty and staff being recognized for their merit and worth (Scriven, 1978)? Are faculty judged on their meritorious contributions as determined by the guild of scholars in one's discipline or field and on the quality of their contributions to the local campus community?

By taking merit and worth into account, these colleges, like all colleges, encounter a tension. On the one hand, they are striving to be more scholarly, which translates into more scholarly publications. These institutions have a strong desire to be recognized by their peers, which is often based on the research activity of the faculty.

On the other hand, these colleges desire to become more rooted with their tradition. They feel it is the right thing to do given the condition of our society (e.g., business practices, decline of community, role of church, and voting patterns). At some colleges, it is squarely based on their religious traditions and commitments to be a force in society. It is also the core of the value-added argument of these colleges, which is becoming more and more important in the highly competitive market for students. Thus they are challenged to balance being both faculty and student centered. Rewarding faculty on merit and worth is one way to practically address this tension, but colleges know that it is a tension to exploit, not eliminate.

Develop a culture and community that honors and promotes open inquiry for all members.

Honor and promote the freedom of inquiry and open exchanges among all members of the campus community, recognizing that it exists within a context of competing forces and perspectives. At these colleges, faculty and their leaders promote and insist on academic freedom—the freedom to explore and create a safe environment for all, including the students—to pursue truth wherever it leads. At the same time, they argue that one begins with a perspective—a worldview—about what is most important to one's life. These unproven assumptions cannot be validated, but they are powerful influences on one's thinking and one's life. As one faculty member stated, "every person moves in a field of biases." For those who hold strong religious "biases," they reconcile this tension by arguing that all truth is God's truth, thus what is there to be afraid of? Others who do not rely on transcendent truth are also very committed to the search for truth, which for them is multiple truths. The task for colleges, then, regardless of their views on the search for truth, is to promote and honor the search. It means giving the freedom for students, faculty, and staff to do so. It is this defining characteristic that makes a college fulfill its primary function—provide open inquiry for all. David Myers, a widely respected professor of psychology at Hope College, offered this perspective:

> God calls us to be witnesses to the truth and to contribute our knowledge to the public spheres of idea. The free market place of ideas is critical in the academy. Because out of the conversations comes greater understanding. I am not always right about the issues I write about, but the process of making public our views for conversation and discussion is the heart of what a college is about.

Faculty see as their charge to develop programs—academic as well as cocurricular—that guide students beyond dogmatism and pure relativism. Faculty can help students realize that there is really no division between their secular and sacred lives and their private faith lives and public pursuit of the good and the true. In short, they can help students progress from a bifurcated to an integrated view of reality and the world in which they live. As we learned, one common and effective way to foster this holistic development is to have as many models as there are faculty and staff to relate to students.

Questions for Campus Conversations

- *How is community defined at your institution that influences how students are guided in their development?*
- *How does your community accept pluralism and diversity based on religion, race, ethnicity, and lifestyle?*
- *What are the challenges in creating a community that simultaneously honors unity and diversity?*
- *How invested are the faculty and staff in forming a unique community(ies) within your institution?*
- *How do faculty and staff collaborate at your institution to develop students holistically?*
- *How do faculty and staff at your institution view their careers in terms of vocation?*
- *Are faculty and staff at your institution rewarded based on their efforts to foster student development holistically?*

Summary

Colleges do invest in students with purpose. They intentionally employ their resources, especially the talents, treasures, and time of their most valued and valuable resources—the faculty and staff—to foster students holistically. These colleges invest through their culture, curriculum, cocurriculum, and communities in and beyond the campus to fulfill their desired end, which can be summarized as developing the "good person." They deeply care about who a student is and becomes, as well as what they will do with their lives.

The 10 institutions we studied prepare students for life beyond college in ways that were very common a century ago, when the student population was more "selective." Career psychologists emphasized the connection between one's personal characteristics—values and purpose as well as aptitudes and skills—and the requirements of the career (Parsons, 1909/1989). Students would benefit by knowing who they are and the expectations of a given career, and by regarding the career as only a part of a calling or vocation. Over the past century, higher education has naturally and appropriately become more career oriented, but in doing so it has not completely followed the advice of the early vocational and career psychologists. Today, this separation is due in part because higher education thinks of itself primarily as professional career preparation. The colleges in our study are at the forefront of questioning this widely held belief. These church colleges regard meaning and purpose not as primarily private matters divorced from intellectual and academic pursuits and from investment in the world to "make a difference." Both are needed to be successful in society, including the world of work. These colleges are concerned about linking career and calling so that graduates will have experiences in critical self-reflection and a language to address their vocation in life. These institutions recognize and support the view that careers are important in the college lives of students, and higher education does not need to deny the centrality of careers in educating students. In fact, they attempt to create an environment for students that can better integrate their careers into their discernment of their purpose in life.

Thus a college education is both an end and a means in the journey of life for students. It has intrinsic and instrumental value, and the individual and society are both beneficiaries. At the colleges we studied, the staff and faculty often referred to college as guiding students in their self-discovery and preparation for making a difference in the world. A good education is not just training for a career but helping students find their calling—in which a career can rightfully play a very important part in living out a life of meaning and purpose. As Sister Ann Ida Gannon, a leader in Catholic higher education for over a half century, has stated, "Having a meaningful life is more important than making a living" (personal communication, August 2005).

We would like to invite you to continue our theme of church-related college involvement in fostering holistic student development by beginning campus conversations about how your college is engaged in putting students first. To help you get started, we end this book with three quotes from notable authors and scholars that express the purpose or desired end of this book: persons (i.e., faculty, staff, and students) can live the good life by learning about and investing their time, treasures, and talents to help this world become a better place to live.

> *"Where your talents and the needs of the world cross, there lies your vocation."*
>
> —Aristotle

> *"The place God calls you to is the place where your deep gladness and the world's deep hunger meet."*
>
> —Frederick Buechner

> *"Good work is what people do in a responsible and personally satisfying way to help meet the needs of society, and thus make this a better world to live in. Good work is apt to occur when the individual and society needs are reinforcing."*
>
> —Howard Gardner, Mihaly Csikszentmihalyi, & William Damon

Bibliography

Abbott, A. (2002, November 21). The aims of education address. *University of Chicago Record, 37*(2), 4–8.

Altbach, P. (1995). Problems and possibilities: The US academic profession. *Studies in Higher Education, 20*(1), 27–44.

American Association for Higher Education, American College Personnel Association, & National Association of Student Personnel Administrators. (1998). *Powerful partnerships: A shared responsibility for learning.* Washington, DC: Authors.

American College Personnel Association & National Association of Student Personnel Administrators. (2004). *Learning reconsidered: A campus-wide focus on the student experience.* Washington, DC: Authors.

American Council on Education. (1994). The student personnel point of view. In A. L. Rentz (Ed.), *Student affairs: A profession's heritage* (2nd ed., pp. 66–77). Lanham, MD: University Press of America. (Original work published 1937)

Association of American Colleges and Universities. (2002). *Greater expectations: A new vision for learning as a nation goes to college.* Washington, DC: Author.

Astin, A. W. (1984). Student involvement: A developmental theory for higher education. *Journal of College Student Personnel, 25,* 297–308.

Astin, A. W. (1993). *What matters in college? Four critical years revisited.* San Francisco, CA: Jossey-Bass.

Astin, A. W. (2004). Why spirituality deserves a central place in higher education. *Spirituality in Higher Education Newsletter, 1*(1). Retrieved September 16, 2005, from http://www.spirituality.ucla.edu/newsletter

Astin, A. W., & Astin, H. S. (1999). *Meaning and spirituality in the lives of college faculty: A study of values, authenticity, and stress.* Los Angeles, CA: Higher Education Research Institute, University of California–Los Angeles.

Austin, A. E. (2002). Preparing the next generation of faculty: Graduate school as socialization to the academic career. *Journal of Higher Education, 73*(1), 94–122.

Austin, A. E. (2003). Creating a bridge to the future: Preparing new faculty to face changing expectations in a shifting context. *Review of Higher Education, 26*(2), 119–144.

Ayers, G. E., & Ray, D. B. (Eds.). (1996). *Service learning: Listening to different voices.* Fairfax, VA: College Fund/UNCF.

Barefoot, B. O., Gardner, J. N., Swing, R. L., & Terenzini, P. (2005). *Effective processes and lessons learned from Foundations of Excellence™ in the first college year: How can we use this for improvement and self-study?* Paper presented at the 110th annual meeting of the Higher Learning Commission, Chicago, IL.

Battistoni, R. M. (2002). *Civic engagement across the curriculum: A resource book for service-learning faculty in all disciplines.* Providence, RI: Campus Compact.

Baxter Magolda, M. B. (1992). *Knowing and reasoning in college: Gender-related patterns in students' intellectual development.* San Francisco, CA: Jossey-Bass.

Baxter Magolda, M. B. (2002). Helping students make their way to adulthood: Good company for the journey. *About Campus, 6*(6), 2–9.

Baxter Magolda, M., & King, P. M. (Eds.). (2004). *Learning partnerships: Theory and models of practice to educate for self-authorship.* Sterling, VA: Stylus.

Benne, R. (2001). *Quality with soul: How six premier colleges and universities keep faith with their religious traditions.* Grand Rapids, MI: Eerdmans.

Bennett, J. B. (2003). *Academic life: Hospitality, ethics, and spirituality.* Bolton, MA: Anker.

Bennett, M. J. (1993). Toward ethnorelativism: A developmental model of intercultural sensitivity. In R. M. Paige (Ed.), *Education for the intercultural experience* (pp. 21–71). Yarmouth, ME: Intercultural Press.

Berberet, J. (2002). Nurturing an ethos of community engagement. In K. J. Zahorski (Ed.), *Scholarship in the postmodern era: New venues, new values, new visions* (pp. 91–100). San Francisco, CA: Jossey-Bass.

Boyer, E. L. (1987). *College: The undergraduate experience in America.* New York, NY: HarperCollins.

Boyer, E. L. (1990a). *Campus life: In search of community.* Princeton, NJ: Carnegie Foundation for the Advancement of Teaching.

Boyer, E. L. (1990b). *Scholarship reconsidered: Priorities of the professoriate.* Princeton, NJ: Carnegie Foundation for the Advancement of Teaching.

Boyer, E. L. (1996). The scholarship of engagement. *Journal of Public Service and Outreach, 1*(1), 11–20.

Braskamp, L. A. (1997). On being responsive and responsible. *CHEA Chronicle, 1*(6). Retrieved September 16, 2005, from http://www.chea.org/Chronicle/vol1/no6/index.cfm

Braskamp, L. A. (2000). Toward a more holistic approach to assessing faculty as teachers. In K. E. Ryan (Ed.), *Evaluating teaching in higher education: A vision for the future* (pp. 19–33). San Francisco, CA: Jossey-Bass.

Braskamp, L. A. (2003). *Fostering student development through faculty development.* Retrieved September 16, 2005, from the Loyola University Chicago web site: www.luc.edu/projectfaculty

Braskamp, L. A., & Hager, M. J. (2005). Personal investment theory: Understanding religious, spiritual, and faith development of students. In M. L. Maehr & S. A. Karabenick (Eds.), *Motivation and religion* (Vol. 14). New York, NY: Elsevier.

Braskamp, L. A., & Ory, J. C. (1994). *Assessing faculty work: Enhancing individual and institutional performance.* San Francisco, CA: Jossey-Bass.

Braskamp, L. A., & Wergin, J. F. (1998). Forming new social partnerships. In W. G. Tierney (Ed.), *The responsive university: Restructuring for high performance* (pp. 62–91). Baltimore, MD: Johns Hopkins University Press.

Brown, R. D. (1972). *Student development in tomorrow's higher education: A return to the academy.* Washington, DC: American College Personnel Association.

Brown, R. D. (1996). We've been there. We've done that. Let's keep it up. *Journal of College Student Development, 37*(2), 239–241.

Buchanan, J. M. (2005, February 20). *To know what we do not know.* Sermon presented at Harvard Memorial Church, Harvard University, Cambridge, MA.

Buechner, F. (1993). *Wishful thinking: A seeker's ABC* (Rev. & expanded ed.). San Francisco, CA: HarperSanFrancisco.

Cantor, N., & Schomberg, S. (2002, November/December). What we want students to learn: Cultivating playfulness and responsibility in a liberal education. *Change, 34*(6), 46–49.

Cantor, N., & Schomberg, S. (2003). Poised between two worlds: The university as monastery and marketplace. *EDUCAUSE Review, 38*(2), 12–21.

Cherry, C., DeBerg, B. A., & Porterfield, A. (2001). *Religion on campus: What religion really means to today's undergraduates.* Chapel Hill, NC: University of North Carolina Press.

Chickering, A. W. (2003, January/February). Reclaiming our soul: Democracy and higher education. *Change, 35*(1), 38–44.

Chickering, A. W., Dalton, J. C., & Stamm, L. (2005). *Encouraging authenticity and spirituality in higher education.* San Francisco, CA: Jossey-Bass.

Chickering, A. W., & Reisser, L. (1993). *Education and identity* (2nd ed.). San Francisco, CA: Jossey-Bass.

Clark, B. R. (1987). *The academic life: Small worlds, different worlds.* Princeton, NJ: Carnegie Foundation for the Advancement of Teaching.

Clark, B. R. (2000, January/February). Collegial entrepreneurialism in proactive universities: Lessons from Europe. *Change, 32*(1), 10–19.

Colby, A., Ehrlich, T., Beaumont, E., & Stephens, J. (2003). *Educating citizens: Preparing America's undergraduates for lives of moral and civic responsibility.* San Francisco, CA: Jossey-Bass.

Connor, W. R. (2005, February 24). *Is liberal education hypocritical?* New York, NY: The Teagle Foundation. Retrieved September 19, 2005, from http://www.teaglefoundation.org/president/entry.aspx?id = 8

Csikszentmihalyi, M. (1997). *Finding flow: The psychology of engagement with everyday life.* New York, NY: Basic Books.

Currie, C. L. (2005, February). The quest for "seamless" student learning. *Connections, 5*(5).

Dalton, J. C., Russell, T. R., & Kline, S. (Eds.). (2004). *New directions for institutional research: No. 22. Assessing character outcomes in college.* San Francisco, CA: Jossey-Bass.

Davenport, F. G. (2004). The Hamline plan: Mentoring, modeling, and monitoring the practical liberal arts. In J. L. Ratcliff, D. K. Johnson, & J. G. Gaff (Eds.), *New directions for higher education: No. 125. Changing general education* (pp. 69–83). San Francisco, CA: Jossey-Bass.

Davis, B. G. (1987). Beyond Ws and Ls: Evaluating intercollegiate athletic programs. In L. A. Braskamp & J. F. Wergin (Eds.), *New directions for institutional research: No. 56. Evaluating administrative services and programs* (pp. 37–48). San Francisco, CA: Jossey-Bass.

DeJong, A. J. (1992). Making sense of church-related higher education. In D. S. Guthrie & R. L. Noftzger (Eds.), *Agendas for church-related colleges and universities* (pp. 19–27). San Francisco, CA: Jossey-Bass.

Denton-Borhaug, K. (2004). The complex and rich landscape of student spirituality: Findings from the Goucher College spirituality survey. *Religion & Education, 31*(2), 21–40.

Dey, E. L., Milem, J. F., & Berger, J. B. (1997). Changing patterns of publication productivity: Accumulative advantage or institutional isomorphism? *Sociology of Education, 70*(4), 308–323.

Diamond, R. M. (1999). *Aligning faculty rewards with institutional mission: Statements, policies, and guidelines.* Bolton, MA: Anker.

Diekema, A. (2000). *Academic freedom and Christian scholarship.* Grand Rapids, MI: Eerdmans.

Donovan, M. S., Bransford, J. D., & Pellegrino, J. W. (1999). *How people learn: Bridging research and practice.* Washington, DC: National Academies Press.

Dovre, P. J. (2001). The future of religious colleges. *Liberal Education, 87*(4), 18–23.

Drummond, S. B. (2005). *Leading change in campus religious life: A case study on the programs for the theological exploration of vocation.* Unpublished doctoral dissertation, University of Wisconsin–Milwaukee.

Dwyer, M. (2004). Charting the impact of studying abroad. *International Educator, 13*(1), 14–20.

Dykstra, C. (1999). *Growing in the life of faith: Education and Christian practices.* Louisville, KY: Geneva Press.

Dykstra, C. (2003). *The theological exploration of vocation.* Plenary address presented at the grant conference for Programs for the Theological Exploration of Vocation, Indianapolis, IN.

Ehrlich, T. (2005). *Service-learning in undergraduate education: Where is it going?* Retrieved September 19, 2005, from http://www.carnegiefoundation.org/perspectives/perspectives2005.July.htm

Estanek, S. M. (2001). Student development and the Catholic university: Philosophical reflections. *Current Issues in Catholic Higher Education, 22*, 37–52.

Eyler, J., & Giles, D. E., Jr. (1999). *Where's the learning in service-learning?* San Francisco, CA: Jossey-Bass.

Ferguson, D. S., & Weston, W. J. (Eds.). (2003). *Called to teach: The vocation of the Presbyterian educator.* Louisville, KY: Geneva Press.

Finsen, L. (2002). Faculty as institutional citizens: Reconceiving service and governance work. In L. A. McMillin & W. G. Berberet (Eds.), *A new academic compact: Revisioning the relationship between faculty and their institutions* (pp. 61–86). Bolton, MA: Anker.

Fish, S. (2005, January 7). One university, under God? *The Chronicle of Higher Education*, p. C1.

Fowler, J. W. (1981). *Stages of faith: The psychology of human development and the quest for meaning.* New York, NY: HarperCollins.

Gaff, J. G. (2004). What is a generally educated person? *Peer Review, 7*(1), 4–7.

Gallop, G., Jr., & Lindsay, D. M. (1999). *Surveying the religious landscape: Trends in U.S. beliefs.* Harrisburg, PA: Morehouse.

Gardner, H., Csikszentmihalyi, M., & Damon, W. (2001). *Good work: When excellence and ethics meet.* New York, NY: Basic Books.

Glassick, C. E., Huber, M. T., & Maeroff, G. I. (1997). *Scholarship assessed: Evaluation of the professoriate.* San Francisco, CA: Jossey-Bass.

Gomes, P. J. (2002). *The good life: Truths that last in times of need.* San Francisco, CA: HarperSanFrancisco.

Guthrie, D. S., & Noftzger, R. L. (Eds.) (1992). *Agendas for church-related colleges and universities.* San Francisco, CA: Jossey-Bass.

Hallie, P. (1979). *Lest innocent blood be shed: The story of the village of Le Chambon and how goodness happened there.* New York, NY: Harper & Row.

Hamrick, F. A., Evans, N. J., & Schuh, J. H. (2002). *Foundations of student affairs practice: How philosophy, theory, and research strengthen educational outcomes.* San Francisco, CA: Jossey-Bass.

Hatch, N. O. (2005, May 6). Intellectual and moral purpose still meet at Catholic universities. *The Chronicle of Higher Education*, p. B16.

Haughey, J. C. (Ed.). (2004). *Revisiting the idea of vocation: Theological explorations.* Washington, DC: The Catholic University of America Press.

Haworth, J. G., & Conrad, C. F. (Eds.). (1995). *Revisioning curriculum in higher education.* Needham Heights, MA: Simon & Schuster.

Heffner, G. G., & Beversluis, C. (Eds.). (2002). *Commitment and connection: Service-learning and Christian higher education.* Lanham, MD: University Press of America.

Heft, J. L., Katsuyama, R. M., & Pestello, F. P. (2001). Faculty attitudes and hiring practices at selected Catholic colleges and universities. *Current Issues in Catholic Higher Education, 21*, 43–63.

Higher Education Research Institute. (2003). *The spiritual life of college students: A national study of college students' search for meaning and purpose.* Los Angeles, CA: Graduate School of Education and Information Studies, University of California–Los Angeles.

Higher Education Research Institute. (2005). *Spirituality in higher education: A national study of college students' search for meaning and purpose.* Los Angeles, CA: Graduate School of Education and Information Studies, University of California–Los Angeles.

Hoekema, D. A. (1994). *Campus rules and moral community: In place of In Loco Parentis.* Lanham, MD: Rowman & Littlefield.

Holcomb, G. L., & Nonneman, A. J. (2004). Faithful change: Exploring and assessing faith development in Christian liberal arts undergraduates. In J. C. Dalton, T. R. Russell, & S. Kline (Eds.), *New directions for institutional research: No. 122. Assessing character outcomes in college* (pp. 93–103). San Francisco, CA: Jossey-Bass.

Howe, N., & Strauss, W. (2003). *Millennials go to college—strategies for a new generation on campus: Recruiting and admissions, campus life, and the classroom.* Great Falls, VA: LifeCourse Associates and American Association of Collegiate Registrars and Admissions Officers.

Huber, M. T. (2002). Faculty evaluation and the development of academic careers. In C. L. Colbeck (Ed.), *New directions for institutional research: No. 114. Evaluating faculty performance* (pp. 73–83). San Francisco, CA: Jossey-Bass.

Hurtado, S., Milem, J., Clayton-Pedersen, A., & Allen, W. (2000). *Enacting diverse learning environments: Improving the climate for racial/ethnic diversity in higher education.* San Francisco, CA: Jossey-Bass.

Jablonski, M. A. (Ed.). (2001). *The implications of student spirituality for student affairs practice.* San Francisco, CA: Jossey-Bass.

Jacobsen D., & Jacobsen, R. H. (2004). *Scholarship and Christian faith: Enlarging the conversation.* New York, NY: Oxford University Press.

Jacoby, B., & Associates. (1996). *Service-learning in higher education: Concepts and practices.* San Francisco, CA: Jossey-Bass.

Johannes, J. R. (2004). [Welcome letter]. *Academics, 1*(1). Retrieved September 19, 2005, from the Villanova University web site: http://www.vpaa.villanova.edu/magazine/vol_1-1.pdf

Katz, S. N. (2005, April 1). Liberal education on the ropes. *The Chronicle of Higher Education*, p. B6.

Kegan, R. (1994). *In over our heads: The mental demands of modern life.* Cambridge, MA: Harvard University Press.

Kellogg Commission on the Future of State and Land-Grant Universities. (1997). *Returning to our roots: The student experience.* Washington, DC: National Association of State Universities and Land-Grant Colleges.

Kennedy, J. C., & Simon, C. J. (2005). *Can Hope endure? A historical case study in Christian higher education.* Grand Rapids, MI: Eerdmans.

Kennedy, W. (1979). *Ironweed.* New York, NY: Penguin Books.

King, P. M., & Kitchener, K. S. (1994). *Developing reflective judgment: Understanding and promoting intellectual growth and critical thinking in adolescents and adults.* San Francisco, CA: Jossey-Bass.

Kohlberg, L. (1976). Moral stages and modernization. In T. Lickona (Ed.), *Moral development and behavior: Theory, research, and social issues* (pp. 31–53). New York, NY: Holt, Rinehart, and Winston.

Kolvenbach, P-H. (2001, Summer). Father general's words on justice in higher education. *Company*, 30–31.

Kouzes, J. M., & Posner, B. Z. (2003). *The Jossey-Bass academic administrator's guide to exemplary leadership.* San Francisco, CA: Jossey-Bass.

Kuh, G. D. (1993). *Cultural perspectives in student affairs work.* Washington, DC: American College Personnel Association.

Kuh, G. D., Kinzie, J., Schuh, J. H., Whitt, E. J., & Associates. (2005). *Student success in college: Creating conditions that matter.* San Francisco, CA: Jossey-Bass and American Association for Higher Education.

Kuh, G. D., Schuh, J. H., Whitt, E. J., & Associates. (1991). *Involving colleges: Successful approaches to fostering student learning and development outside the classroom.* San Francisco, CA: Jossey-Bass.

Kuh, G. D., & Whitt, E. J. (1988). *The invisible tapestry: Culture in American colleges and universities.* Washington, DC: Association for the Study of Higher Education.

Lagemann, E. C. (2003). The challenge of liberal education: Past, present, and future. *Liberal Education, 89*(2), 6–13.

Levine, L. W. (1998, March 6). Struggles are a small price to pay for diverse universities. *The Chronicle of Higher Education*, p. B4.

Lindholm, J. (2003). Perceived organizational fit: Nurturing the minds, hearts, and personal ambitions of university faculty. *Review of Higher Education, 27*(1), 125–149.

Lindholm, J. (2004). Pathways to the professoriate: The role of self, others, and environment in shaping academic career aspirations. *Journal of Higher Education, 75*(6), 603–635.

Love, P. G. (2002). Comparing spiritual development and cognitive development. *Journal of College Student Development, 43*(3), 357–373.

MacKinnon-Slaney, F. (1993). Theory to practice in cocurricular activities: A new model for student involvement. *College Student Affairs Journal, 12*(2), 35–40.

Maehr, M. L., & Braskamp, L. A. (1986). *The motivation factor: A theory of personal investment.* Lexington, MA: Lexington Books.

Mahoney, K. A., Schmalzbauer, J., & Youniss, J. (2001). Religion: A comeback on campus. *Liberal Education, 87*(4), 36–41.

Mannoia, V. J., Jr. (2000). *Christian liberal arts: An education that goes beyond.* Lanham, MD: Rowman & Littlefield.

Marsden, G. M. (1994). *The soul of the American university: From Protestant establishment to established nonbelief.* New York, NY: Oxford University Press.

Marsden, G. M. (2002). Beyond progressive scientific humanism. In P. J. Dovre (Ed.), *The future of religious colleges* (pp. 35–50). Grand Rapids, MI: Eerdmans.

Marty, M. E. (2000). *Education, religion, and the common good: Advancing a distinctly American conversation about religion's role in our shared life.* San Francisco, CA: Jossey-Bass.

McDonald, W. M. (2002). Absent voices: Assessing students' perceptions of campus community. In W. M. McDonald & Associates, *Creating campus community: In search of Ernest Boyer's legacy* (pp. 145–168). San Francisco, CA: Jossey-Bass.

Migliazzo, A. C. (Ed.). (2002). *Teaching as an act of faith: Theory and practice in church-related higher education.* Bronx, NY: Fordham University Press.

Milem, J. F., Berger, J. B., & Dey, E. L. (2000). Faculty time allocation: A study of change over twenty years. *Journal of Higher Education, 71*(4), 454–475.

Miller V. M., & Ryan, M. M. (Eds.). (2001). *Transforming campus life: Reflections on spirituality and religious pluralism.* New York, NY: Peter Lang.

Miller, W. R. (2004). What is human nature? Reflections from Judeo-Christian perspectives. In W. R. Miller & H. D. Delaney (Eds.), *Judeo-Christian perspectives on psychology: Human nature, motivation, and change* (pp. 11–30). Washington, DC: American Psychological Association.

Morton, K. (1995). The irony of service: Charity, project, and social change in service learning. *Michigan Journal of Community Service Learning, 2*, 19–32.

Nash, R. J. (2001). *Religious pluralism in the academy: Opening the dialogue.* New York, NY: Peter Lang.

Nash, R. J. (2002). *Spirituality, ethics, religion, and teaching: A professor's journey*. New York, NY: Peter Lang.

National Survey of Student Engagement. (2004). *Student engagement: Pathways to collegiate success.* Bloomington, IN: Center for Postsecondary Research, Indiana University Bloomington.

Neafsey, J. P. (2004). Psychological dimensions of the discernment of vocation. In J. C. Haughey (Ed.), *Revisiting the idea of vocation: Theological explorations* (pp. 163–195). Washington, DC: The Catholic University of America Press.

Niebuhr, H. R. (1951). *Christ and culture.* New York, NY: Harper & Row.

Nuss, E. M. (1996). The development of student affairs. In S. R. Komives, D. B. Woodard, Jr., & Associates, *Student services: A handbook for the profession* (pp. 22–42). San Francisco, CA: Jossey-Bass.

Oakley, F. (2002). Concluding reflections on the Lilly seminar. In A. Sterk (Ed.), *Religion, scholarship, and higher education: Perspectives, models, and future prospects* (pp. 231–246). Notre Dame, IN: University of Notre Dame Press.

O'Meara, K. A., & Braskamp, L. A. (2005). Aligning faculty reward systems and development to promote faculty and student growth. *NASPA Journal, 42*(2), 223–240.

O'Toole, J. (2005). *Creating the good life: Applying Aristotle's wisdom to find meaning and happiness.* New York, NY: Rodale.

Palmer, P. J. (1987). Community, conflict, and ways of knowing: Ways to deepen our educational agenda. *Change, 19*(5), 20–25.

Palmer, P. J. (1990). *The active life: A spirituality of work, creativity, and caring.* San Francisco, CA: HarperSanFrancisco.

Palmer, P. J. (1993). *The promise of paradox: Celebration of contradictions in the Christian life.* Washington, DC: The Servant Leadership School.

Palmer, P. J. (1998). *The courage to teach: Exploring the inner landscape of a teacher's life.* San Francisco, CA: Jossey-Bass.

Parks, S. D. (2000). *Big questions, worthy dreams: Mentoring young adults in their search for meaning, purpose, and faith.* San Francisco, CA: Jossey-Bass.

Parsons, F. (1989). *Choosing a vocation.* Garrett Park, MD: Garrett Park Press. (Original work published 1909)

Pascarella, E. T., & Terenzini, P. T. (1991). *How college affects students: Findings and insights from twenty years of research.* San Francisco, CA: Jossey-Bass.

Pascarella, E. T., & Terenzini, P. T. (2005). *How college affects students: A third decade of research* (Vol. 2). San Francisco, CA: Jossey-Bass.

Pascarella, E. T., Wolniak, G. C., Cruce, T. M., & Blaich, C. F. (2004). Do liberal arts colleges really foster good practices in undergraduate education? *Journal of College Student Development, 45*(1), 57–74.

Perry, W. G. (1968). *Forms of intellectual and ethical development in the college years: A scheme.* New York, NY: Holt, Rinehart, and Winston.

Poe, H. L. (2004). *Christianity in the academy: Teaching at the intersection of faith and learning.* Grand Rapids, MI: Baker Academic.

Putnam, R. D. (2000). *Bowling alone: The collapse and revival of American community.* New York, NY: Simon & Schuster.

Rice, R. E. (1996). *Making a place for the new American scholar.* Washington, DC: American Association for Higher Education.

Rice, R. E. (2002). Beyond *Scholarship Reconsidered:* Toward an enlarged vision of the scholarly work of faculty members. In K. J. Zahorski (Ed.), *Scholarship in the postmodern era: New venues, new values, new visions* (pp. 7–18). San Francisco, CA: Jossey-Bass.

Riley, N. S. (2005). *God on the quad: How religious colleges and the missionary generation are changing America.* New York, NY: St. Martin's Press.

Sanford, N. (1962). Developmental status of the entering freshman. In N. Sanford (Ed.), *The American college: A psychological and social interpretation of the higher learning* (pp. 253–282). New York, NY: Wiley.

Sanford, N. (1967). *Where colleges fail: A study of the student as a person.* San Francisco, CA: Jossey-Bass.

Schmeltekopf, D. D., & Vitanza, D. M. (Eds.). (2003). *The Baptist and Christian character of Baylor.* Waco, TX: Baylor University.

Schwartz, A. (2001). Growing spiritually during the college years. *Liberal Education, 87*(4), 30–35.

Schwehn, M. R. (1993). *Exiles from Eden: Religion and the academic vocation in America.* New York, NY: Oxford University Press.

Scriven, M. (1978). Value versus merit. *Evaluation News, 8*, 1–3.

Shaara, M. (1987). *The killer angels.* New York, NY: Ballantine Books.

Shinn, L. D. (2004, January/February). A conflict of cultures: Governance at liberal arts colleges. *Change, 36*(1), 18–26.

Shulman, L. S. (2002, November/December). Making differences: A table of learning. *Change, 34*(6), 36–44.

Shulman, L. S. (2004). *Teaching as community property: Essays on higher education.* San Francisco, CA: Jossey-Bass.

Simon, C. J., Bloxham, L., Doyle, D., Hailey, M., Hawks, J. H., Light, K., et al. (2003). *Mentoring for mission: Nurturing new faculty at church-related colleges.* Grand Rapids, MI: Eerdmans.

Sloan, D. (1994). *Faith and knowledge: Mainline Protestantism and American higher education.* Louisville, KY: Westminster John Knox Press.

Smith, D. G., & Schonfeld, N. B. (2000). The benefits of diversity: What the research tells us. *About Campus, 5*(5), 16–23.

Stake, R. E. (2004). *Standards-based and responsive evaluation.* Thousand Oaks, CA: Sage.

Stark, J. S., & Lattuca, L. R. (1997). Defining curriculum: An academic plan. In J. S. Stark & L. R. Lattuca (Eds.), *Shaping the college curriculum: Academic plans in action* (pp. 7–21). Needham Heights, MA: Allyn & Bacon.

Storm, K. (2004). *Pragmatism.* Spokane, WA: Whitworth College.

Tierney, W. G., & Bensimon, E. M. (1996). *Promotion and tenure: Community and socialization in academe.* Albany, NY: State University of New York Press.

Tisdell, E. J. (2003). *Exploring spirituality and culture in adult and higher education.* San Francisco, CA: Jossey-Bass.

Trautvetter, L. C. (1999). Experiences of women, experiences of men. In R. J. Menges & Associates, *Faculty in new jobs: A guide to settling in, becoming established, and building institutional support* (pp. 59–87). San Francisco, CA: Jossey-Bass.

Ward, K. (2003). *Faculty service roles and the scholarship of engagement.* San Francisco, CA: Jossey-Bass.

Ward, K., & Wolf-Wendel, L. (2000). Community-centered service learning: Moving from doing for to doing with. *American Behavioral Scientist, 43*(5), 767–780.

Weisser, S. O. (2005). "Believing in yourself" as classroom culture. *Academe, 91*(1), 27–31.

Wellman, J. (2003). *Religious scholarship and insider status: The question of teaching and faith.* Retrieved September 20, 2005, from the Loyola University Chicago web site: http://www.luc.edu/project faculty/pdf/wellman.pdf

Wergin, J. F. (2003). *Departments that work: Building and sustaining cultures of excellence in academic programs.* Bolton, MA: Anker.

Willimon, W. H., & Naylor, T. H. (1995). *The abandoned generation: Rethinking higher education.* Grand Rapids, MI: Eerdmans.

Wolf-Wendel, L., & Ward, K. (in press). Academic motherhood: Variations by institutional type. *Higher Education.*

Wolfe, A. (2002, February 8). Faith and diversity in American religion. *The Chronicle of Higher Education*, p. B7.

Wolterstorff, N. (2002). Epilogue. In A. Sterk (Ed.), *Religion, scholarship, and higher education: Perspectives, models, and future prospects* (pp. 247–254). Notre Dame, IN: University of Notre Dame Press.

Wulff, D. H., Austin, A. E., & Associates. (2004). *Paths to the professorate: Strategies for enriching the preparation of future faculty.* San Francisco, CA: Jossey-Bass.

Wuthnow, R. (2004). *Can faith be more than a side show in the contemporary academy?* Paper presented at the Faith in the Academy conference, Messiah College, Grantham, PA.

Zachman, R. C. (2003). *The challenge of teaching theology to those who believe.* Retrieved September 20, 2005, from the Loyola University Chicago web site: http://www.luc.edu/projectfaculty/pdf/teachingtheology.pdf

Zlotkowski, E. (Ed.). (1998). *Successful service-learning programs: New models of excellence in higher education.* Bolton, MA: Anker.

Index